Growth & Welfare, in the American Past

second edition

Growth & Welfare in the American Past

a new economic history **Douglass C. North**

University of Washington

PRENTICE-HALL, INC.   *Englewood Cliffs, N.J.*

Library of Congress Cataloging in Publication Data

NORTH, DOUGLASS CECIL.
  Growth and welfare in the American past.

  Bibliography: p. 178
  1. United States—Economic conditions. I. Title.
HC103.N6 1974   330.9'73   73–5531
ISBN 0-13-365338-2

Growth and Welfare in the American Past, second edition
by Douglass C. North

Prentice-Hall International, Inc., London
Prentice-Hall of Australia, Pty. Ltd., Sydney
Prentice-Hall of Canada, Ltd., Toronto
Prentice-Hall of India Private Limited, New Delhi
Prentice-Hall of Japan, Inc., Tokyo

CONTENTS

PREFACE

This edition is an extensive overhauling of the first, a substantial rewriting made possible—even necessary—by the vitality of economic history since 1966 (the first publication date). Recent research has confirmed, expanded, modified, and in some cases contradicted the findings of the first edition. The second edition takes all this into account and keeps its original objective: to present, in the light of the best and latest research, a nontechnical reappraisal of America's economic experience.

An equally important objective is to point the way to restructuring historical enquiry by a systematic use of tools of the social sciences. Indeed, much of the new research in economics and economic history attempts to provide a frame of reference broader than traditional economic theory; the new research treads borderlines of political and social theory. Accordingly, this edition incorporates analysis of institutional change and decision making via the political process, in an attempt to provide a more unified explanation of the American experience. In a very real sense this new emphasis brings the new economic history closer to the more traditional framework of the historian who emphasized the political, legal, and social environment within which economic decisions were made. The difference is that, as in the case of the new economic history, a unified, consistent theoretical approach is the objective, rather than *ad hoc* and unique explanations. Immense historical knowledge is still an essential prerequisite, and we keep adding to the theoretical tools that the economic historian must master.

The organization of the book remains the same. I have necessarily continued to be selective in such a short book. The early chapters do attempt to provide an overview of the issues and the economy's development. Thereafter, I have followed the presentation though not necessarily the subject matter of the previous edition; i.e., a general description and analysis of a period or specific subject and then exploration of a major issue in the history of the American economy.

I am indebted to many scholars who have used the first edition and have taken the trouble to suggest changes, which I have incorporated in this edition. Gary Walton made many detailed suggestions. My main debt, however, is to my colleague Bob Higgs who not only made detailed suggestions chapter by chapter, but also has read and vastly improved this new draft. While I can't blame him for the errors, he deserves much of the credit for the improvements.

ABBREVIATIONS USED IN
CITATIONS OF PUBLISHED WORKS

AER	*American Economic Review*
AHR	*American Historical Review*
EDCC	*Economic Development and Cultural Change*
EHR	*Economic History Review*
GPO	U.S. Government Printing Office
Hist. Statistics	U.S. Bureau of the Census, *Historical Statistics of the United States, Colonial Times to 1957*
ICHS	*The International Congress of the Historical Sciences*
IEAC	International Economic Association Conference
JEH	*Journal of Economic History*
JP	*Journal of Philosophy*
JPE	*Journal of Political Economy*
NBER	National Bureau of Economic Research
SEJ	*Southern Economic Journal*
U.S. Cong. JEC	U.S. Congress Joint Economic Committee

FIGURES

TABLES

Growth & Welfare in the American Past

THEORY, STATISTICS, AND HISTORY

Economic history focuses on two main issues: one is the economic growth, stagnation, or decline of a society; the other is what happens to people within the society in the course of such growth, stagnation, or decline. The latter issue is a consideration of the relative economic welfare of groups. If, as a society grew richer, everyone's income were to grow at the same rate, this would not be a vital question. But we know that in the course of growth some groups fare better than others. On occasion, even in a prospering society, the income of some parts of the society may actually be dropping.

In looking at these two issues, we want to be sure that our analysis takes into account *all* the benefits and costs of the events we examine; that is, were there side effects that were not properly measured in our calculations? For example, in examining nineteenth-century growth and the concomitant industrialization, have we taken into account the harmful effects of pollution and unsanitary conditions that existed in the new industrial cities? Environmental effects are not new phenomena, but they have frequently been neglected by economic historians.

In examining the American experience, then, we are going to ask what factors influenced (1) the rate of growth of the economy and (2) the well-being of various segments of its society, as the country grew.

In order to talk meaningfully about growth and welfare, it is necessary to use economic theory and statistics. It is impossible to analyze and explain the issues dealt with in economic history without developing initial hypotheses and testing them in the light of available evidence. The initial hypotheses come from the body of economic theory that has evolved in the past 200 years and is being continually tested and refined by empirical inquiry. The statistics provide the precise measurement and empirical evidence by which to test the theory. *The inquiry is limited only by the existence of appropriate theory and evidence.* Of course, the development of new theories or the discovery of new evidence permits us to push out the limits, to make sense of events that were previously inexplicable.

Existing economic theory is appropriate for a broad range of issues in economic history dealing with welfare. Since the theory has been tested and retested in innumerable empirical inquiries, it is a short cut distilled from previous research. Testing hypotheses may may lead to rejecting or modifying them in the light of evidence, but the first essential step in exploring a welfare issue is drawn from the body of economic theory.

In the study of economic growth, however, the theory is far from completely adequate. Nevertheless, the development of hypotheses about economic growth in the past twenty years has been a major part of research in economics and has revolutionary implications for the reappraisal of all economic history. Future studies of economic growth will surely provide new fuel for economic historians, but we already have sufficient applicable theory for a start, as the brief distillation in the next section will illustrate.

The evidence is, ideally, statistical data that precisely define and measure the variables at issue. The immense development of such data in American economic history in the past twenty-five years has made possible a revolution in economic history, even though it is still a long way from providing all the information we would like to have, as many of the subsequent chapters will testify. It is a Utopian dream to expect that the economic historian will ever have all the precise quantitative information required to test all his theories (although diligent digging has yielded, and promises to yield, a much richer mine of it than was expected in both the near and the distant past), and here the more imprecise and traditional evidence of the historian found in diaries, records, and other literary sources must be carefully mined. The important point to keep in mind is that such evidence is a poor substitute for precise measurement, and the historian must be self-conscious about the weights he assigns to such qualitative information.

Extensive and intensive growth

The reason for the economic historian's concern with the overall growth of society should be apparent. How well off people can be within a society depends on how many goods and services that society produces. Going back two hundred years or less, we discover that most people lived poorly (by modern Western standards). Their society simply did not produce very much. It was therefore impossible for more than a very small segment of the population to have high living standards—a condition that still characterizes a large part of the world today. The importance of increasing productive capacity cannot be overemphasized. Redistributing income or eliminating depressions would result in less gain for the poor or the whole society than they would derive from even a relatively short period of sustained economic growth. The consequences of a compounded real per capita growth rate of 1.6 percent per year dwarf all other welfare effects in our history. The prime issue to be understood, then, is how the Western world—a small part of the whole—achieved growth that makes possible a standard of life undreamed of in past centuries.

The term *economic growth* has two distinct meanings. When people say that a city or region grows, they usually mean that the number of people and the amount of business activity increase. There is an increase in output because more people, capital, and land are being put to productive use. This is sometimes called *extensive* growth. It has always been a major aspect of America's development. In the eighteenth and nineteenth centuries the territorial boundaries of the United States were filled out; foreign capital and millions of people came from foreign shores to help in the process.

This *extensive* growth meant an increase in the output of goods and services, but it did not necessarily mean the growth of output *per head*—and that is the crucial aspect of growth, the meaning that economists usually employ, because it is concerned with how well off people are. A society is materially better off only if it produces more

TABLE I·1   PER CAPITA GNP 1969 (in U.S. dollars)

$0–100   31% of world population

Borundi	Rwanda	Iran
Botswana	Seychelles Is.	Maldive Is.
Chad	Somalia	Nepal
Dahomey	Tanzania	Sikkim
Ethiopia	Upper Volta	Yemen (Arab Republic)
Guinea	Zaire	
Lesotho		Haiti
Malawi	Afghanistan	
Mali	Bhutan	
Niger	Burma	Indonesia
Nigeria	China	Portuguese Timor

$101–300   32.7% of world population

Algeria	U.A.R.	Thailand
Angola	Zambia	Yemen (Democratic)
Cameroon		
Central African Republic	Cape Verde Is.	Cuba
Congo	Comoro Is.	Dominica
Gabon	Equatorial Guinea	Dominican Republic
Ghana	Gambia	El Salvador
Ivory Coast	São Tomé and Príncipe	Granada
Kenya	Spanish Sahara	Honduras
Liberia		St. Kitts-Nevis-Anguilla
Malagasy Republic	Ceylon	St. Lucia
Mauritania	India	St. Vincent
Mauritius	Jordan	
Morocco	Khmer	Bolivia
Mozambique	Laos	Brazil
Portuguese Guinea	Macao	Colombia
Rhodesia	North Korea	Ecuador
Senegal	Oman Pakistan	Paraguay
Sierra Leone	Philippines	
Sudan	Republic of Korea	British Solomon Is.
Togo	Republic of Vietnam	Fiji
Tunisia	Syria	Papua New Guinea
Uganda	Taiwan	Western Samoa

$301–600   5.9% of world population

Ceuta and Melilla	Portugal	Chile
French Territory of Afars	Turkey	Guyana
and Issas	Yugoslavia	Peru
		Surinam
Bahrain	Antigua	Uruguay
Iran	Barbados	
Iraq	British Honduras	
Lebanon	Costa Rica	American Samoa
Malaysia	Guadeloupe	Gilbert and Ellice Is.
Mongolia	Guatemala	New Hebrides
Saudi Arabia	Jamaica	Tonga
	Mexico	Trust Territories of
Albania	Nicaragua	the Pacific Is.

$601–1200   11.8% of world population

Brunei	Bulgaria	Ireland	Martinique
Hong Kong	Channel Is.	Malta	Panama
Réunion	Gibraltar	Poland	
Ryukuy Is.	Greece	Romania	
Singapore	Greenland	Spain	Argentina
South Africa	Hungary	U.S.S.R.	French Guiana

$1201 plus   18.6% of world population

Israel	Germany (West)	Isle of Man	Puerto Rico
Japan	Italy	Luxembourg	United States
Kuwait	Sweden	Norway	Virgin Is.
Qatar	United Kingdom	Switzerland	
Austria			Australia
Belgium	Denmark	Bermuda	French Polynesia
Czechoslovakia	Faeroe Is.	Canada	Guam
France	Finland	Canal Zone	New Caledonia
Germany (East)	Iceland	Netherlands Antilles	New Zealand

Source: *World Bank Atlas: Population, Per Capita Product and Growth Rates* (Washington, D.C.: IBRD 1971).

output per person.[1] This *intensive* growth, or the growth of individual material well-being, can come about only if output grows at a more rapid rate than population does.[2] Before examining the sources of increasing per capita output (and its counterpart, the income people receive for producing that output, or income per capita) it is well to remember that scarcity is man's oldest problem. By necessity, it has been the dominant feature of life on this planet ever since the beginning. Man has had to scratch out a living through most of the known past, and the degree to which he has climbed above subsistence has been limited indeed. Most of history has been a story of man getting just barely enough to survive. But the last two centuries have seen a dramatic change in which, in the Western world and particularly in the United States, man has soared above this level. Today, hunger, famine, and subsistence are not major American problems, as they have been for most of man's history and continue to be in many parts of the world.

Table I.1 shows that the per capita output of most of the world is still very low. The figures were arrived at by taking the total income of each country, dividing by its population, then translating from that country's currency into equivalent dollars. Many limitations are inherent in this method of making intercountry comparisons (including nonmeasurement of the "side effects" mentioned in the second paragraph), but it gives a rough approximation of comparative levels of living and illustrates that only a very small percentage of the world lives by a standard that most Americans would consider even crudely comfortable. If a dividing line of $600 annually per head is set as a rough approximation, more than two-thirds of the world's population lives below this level, and it is primarily the countries of the Western world that have greatly exceeded it (Japan and the oil sheikdoms are the main exceptions).

What accounts for this phenomenon—that the United States and a small part of the world have been so successful, and the rest of the world relatively ineffectual, in achieving a high standard of living?

[1] An important alternative is additional leisure. People choose more leisure in the form of a shorter workweek, and the decline in the workweek in the United States from approximately 70 hours to about 40 hours reflects a desire to substitute more leisure for additional output and income.

[2] This suggests the further complication of an increase in population in response to rising income. In many parts of the world there has been a Malthusian response to increasing total output, so that output per head has not increased.

This book is a case study of the country that has reached notable heights in this pursuit. Economic growth essentially means increasing productivity— that is, what makes a country grow and become better off per head is that it produces more output per person; therefore, when we talk about growth, we are concentrating on what makes a society more productive. And what makes a society more productive comprises four main features.

The first of these is technological progress; the second is investment in people or, to use the economist's term, investment in human capital; the third is investment in material capital; and the fourth is improvements in the efficiency of economic organization. Because this last feature is so important and underlies the amount of investment in the first three, it will be treated separately in Chapter II.

Technological progress

Technological progress has been the main answer of economic historians in talking about the success of the Western world. The Industrial Revolution has been viewed as a kind of watershed in man's experience; on the far side of it, man was doomed to live at low levels of income, while on the near side, substantially higher standards of life have been attainable.

A man of two hundred years ago would have been more at home a thousand or even fifteen hundred years earlier than he would be in our day. In the past two centuries, man's life has been transformed incalculably by radical changes in technology: (1) the substitution of machines for man's hands to undertake projects—and this is one that Adam Smith made famous in his early discussion in *The Wealth of Nations;* (2) the development of new sources of energy, of which the most famous was the development of the steam engine in the Industrial Revolution period, but more recent examples are the internal combustion engine, the turbine and hydroelectric power, and modern nuclear power; and (3) the dramatic and revolutionary advances in transforming matter to make it useful for mankind, such as transmuting ubiquitous, workaday coal into luxury textiles and fabrics.

A moment's reflection, however, should suggest that the technological source of growth alone is not a sufficient explanation of the unique experience of the United States, since technical knowledge is available to everyone at small cost. Anyone who wants to use modern technology needs only to read the scientific journals, to borrow from the most advanced countries doing research.[3] Therefore, if technological progress were the whole story of economic growth, all the countries in the world should be rich. As a matter of fact, what has happened is that countries have not been able to make efficient use of this technology—they could not reach the potential that is evident in real life in the Western world, and in America particularly, because they lack the other three essentials: human capital that is capable of adapting, modifying, and using technology; physical capital in which the technology is embodied; and efficient economic organization.

Investment in human and physical capital

Highly complicated modern technology requires its users to possess vast amounts of education, or "investment in human capital." First must come the training of engineers and scientists who will modify and adapt it to the particular needs of the different countries; since each country has different resource endowments and different prices at which labor and capital work, what is an ideal technique for one country needs modification for another.[4] Second, this technology must be widely employed, requiring a labor force with sufficient education and training to make efficient use of complex machinery and techniques. And third, as society becomes more complex (as in urban industrial economies like the United States in modern times), a vast array of educated professional people is needed to carry out the demanding tasks of a highly interrelated society. Most underdeveloped areas simply do not have these prerequisities. Before they can make good use of modern technology, they must make substantial investments in education. As economists would say, there is complementarity between physical capital (that is, plant, equipment, machinery) and human capital, which is the sum of people's accumulated productive

---

[3] There is still no overall theory of technological change, although some interesting hypotheses have emerged in recent research. Note, however, that it is one problem to explain fundamental advances in technology and still another to explain the spread of existing technological knowledge.

[4] For example, a machine is made in America in light of the fact that labor may cost $3.00 an hour; therefore, the machine is designed to economize on labor. Such a machine may not be the most efficient type in India, where labor costs are a small fraction of U.S. costs, but the machine is just as expensive as it is in the United States.

attributes—acquired not only through formal education in schools and colleges but also from informal education in on-the-job training, in apprenticeship programs, in maintaining good health, and in all the variety of other ways by which people may make better use of their abilities.

The complementarity between human and physical capital already suggests that investment in material capital plays an important role in economic growth. It is one thing to develop new techniques, still another thing to train people and to build machines to take advantage of these new techniques. Thus, just as we need investment in education and on-the-job training, we need investment in plant, machinery, and equipment. Together, the trained human beings and the material capital can efficiently exploit the new techniques available to man.

Investment in research to discover new techniques, in human beings, and in plant and equipment (material capital) requires savings—and savings represent forgone present consumption. Economic growth, therefore, requires that people be encouraged to forgo present consumption and save part of their income. People and governments (at the state as well as the federal level) invest in university research; firms invest in research; parents send their children to schools and colleges; individuals invest in their own training; and firms borrow money from banks (where individuals have deposited their savings) to expand plant and equipment. We take these characteristics of our world for granted. But we should not. They are integral parts of the growth process that developed in our economy but has been conspicuously lacking in much of the world—as we shall see in the next chapter.

The growth process may be summarized as increased productivity, resulting from increased output from land, labor, capital, and managerial talent. Productivity can be increased through better machines and tools (new ideas embodied in new capital equipment), better educated and trained labor (human capital investment), improvements in the organization of markets. It can also come about when people shift from poor land to better land or from low-productivity to high-productivity occupations (e.g., from agriculture to manufacturing in the nineteenth century). All of these sources of improving productivity have been important in America's past and will come in for more attention in later chapters.

Growth and employment

It is important to distinguish carefully between the economics of growth and that of full employment. Growth is concerned with productive capacity; employment, with the degree to which that capacity is utilized. Although the economics of growth has dominated the foregoing analysis, the extent to which resources are employed is also obviously important to the overall welfare of a society. Unemployed resources represent unused capacity, which means not only lower income than the society is capable of attaining, but also, for labor in particular, it means unemployed workers with all the attendant hardships and distress that accompany depression periods.

Our history is characterized by recurring periods of unemployment. They are endemic to a market economy in which the level of economic activity is the sum of the individual decisions of entrepreneurs and consumers. But the degree of inevitable fluctuations in income and the amount by which we fall short of full employment can be mitigated by an efficient banking system and by appropriate monetary and fiscal policies of the federal government. An efficient banking system not only makes the capital market work smoothly (channeling savings into investment) but also affects the supply of money, which is one of the major influences upon fluctuation in income.[5] Fiscal and monetary policies of the federal government influence how much people will spend and therefore can significantly modify fluctuations, but it is only in the past two decades that fiscal and monetary policies of our federal government have been consistently directed toward a policy of full employment—although not always with complete success, as our recent history makes abundantly clear.

[5] A major issue of economic theory of the past decade has been the importance of the money supply as a determinant of economic activity. That the two sides are not really as far apart as the noise of the controversy suggests is made clear in a monumental study by Milton Friedman and Anna Schwartz, *A Monetary History of the United States, 1867–1960* (Princeton, N.J.: Princeton Univ., 1963), and in reviews by leading critics of the monetary school. Especially see James Tobin, "The Monetary Interpretation of History," *AER*, LV, No. 3 (June 1965), pp. 464–85. However, the recent era of inflation coupled with a substantial level of unemployment makes clear that the issues of macroeconomic theory are far from settled.

NOTE: *AER*, the abbreviation for *American Economic Review* is typical of abbreviations used throughout the footnotes and source lines for tables and charts. A complete list with full titles appears in the front matter.

Welfare: the distribution of income

Unemployment can scarcely be mentioned without thinking of the economic historian's second major concern: welfare—literally, how well did any group fare in its economic setting? In overall terms, the welfare of all groups is reflected in the distribution of income in the society, and changes in this income distribution will mirror shifts in the relative well-being of different groups. Many of the major issues that confront the economic historian concern the real or alleged improvement or deterioration in the income position of a segment of the society. The standard of life of the worker during the Industrial Revolution, the discontent of the farmer in the late nineteenth century, and the anti-poverty campaign in modern times are examples of such issues. Accurate quantitative data are necessary to measure the actual change in the income status of any group, and economic analysis is required to provide an explanation for changes in relative material well-being.

Does the explanation fit the facts?

Explanation of issues of welfare and growth, therefore, comes from economic analysis, and these explanations are tested by determining the extent to which they provide a "best fit" to the available evidence. Sometimes when issues of welfare and growth are raised, they can be directly resolved by accurate and precise measurements. For example, it is commonly asserted that the more rapid fall of farm prices, compared to the prices of other goods in the last third of the nineteenth century, was one of the causes of agrarian discontent. Another common assertion is that the Civil War accelerated the economic growth of the United States and made possible its industrialization.

The role of farm prices in agrarian discontent can be ascertained by getting good price indices of agricultural and other commodities during this period. Surprisingly, the available data show that agricultural prices did not fall more rapidly than other prices. The effect of the Civil War can be examined critically by getting data on the rate of growth of the American economy and on the growth of manufacturing output. These show that the economy grew most rapidly in the decades before and after the Civil War, but very slowly in the war decade. Manufacturing output had already been growing very rapidly before the war; and indeed, by any standards we were already a great industrial nation. Therefore, neither assertion will withstand the test of examination in the light of readily available statistics.

A more common assertion that defies simple statistical testing, however, is that the society or the groups were better off or worse off than they would have been had "circumstances" been different. In subsequent chapters, we shall examine the following familiar statements about the welfare of groups or the American society as a whole in American history.

British policy was vindictive and injurious to the colonial economy after 1763.

The railroad was indispensable for American economic growth.

Speculators and railroads (through land grants) monopolized the best western lands in the nineteenth century, slowed down the westward movement, adversely affected the growth of the economy, and favored the rich over the poor.

In the era of the robber barons, farmers and workers were exploited.

These statements are really incomplete. If we are to make any accurate appraisals of the issues and of the welfare implications, we may rephrase them to read more properly.

British policies were restrictive and injurious to the colonial economy after 1763, compared to what would have taken place had the colonies been independent during these years; or more precisely, income of the Colonies under British rule after 1763 was less than it would have been had the colonists been free and independent.

Income in the United States would have been reduced more than 10 percent had there been no railroads in 1890.

A different (but specified) land policy would have led to more rapid westward settlement in the nineteenth century, a higher rate of economic growth, and a more equal distribution of income.

In the absence of the monopolistic practices of the robber barons, farm income and real wages of manufacturing workers would have been significantly higher.

There are three essential ingredients in this analysis. First, the alternative being hypothesized must be reasonable. It would not make sense to hypothesize a world of free trade as the alternative against which to measure colonial income, since that was simply not the likely alternative in the world of 1763–1775. Second, to construct the hypothetical alternative we must use economic theory and analysis to understand how an economy does operate and how it would have operated under different conditions. Third, good statistical data are necessary to measure what actual income was, compared to the hypothetical income to be developed in the hypothetical alternative. I do not mean to suggest that this method resolves all problems in measuring relative welfare of people in our past. We may disagree about what is a reasonable alternative. We may even argue about the quality of the economic analysis used in creating the hypothetical alternative. And finally, we may not have the statistical data to measure accurately what the difference was. There is no way to avoid using the hypothetical alternative in economic history, since it is implicit in every statement involving causation; but seven years of controversy on this issue since the publication of the first edition of this book have made clear the numerous pitfalls in such analysis. In order to have an unequivocal answer to the question posed by the hypothetical alternative, we may need a general equilibrium model that tells us not only how everything would have been different at the moment of time we are examining the issue, but also how this difference would have affected subsequent growth and welfare in the economy. This is simply beyond the capacity of economic theory and all we can do is try to come as close to this ideal as theory and evidence permit us.[6]

One additional point should be stressed. What actually happened to people, and what people thought happened, were frequently not the same thing. For example, with hindsight it may turn out that the American colonists fared rather well under English rule and, indeed, that they would not have fared as well under alternative possibilities. But the colonists, acting upon the view that they would be

---

[6] There is nothing novel about the use of the hypothetical alternative. The welfare statements cited above are all paraphrases of familiar statements made by historians, and historical writings are replete with similar assertions. The novelty is in turning such assertions into testable propositions, and this necessarily involves the methods described above. The concept of counterfactual propositions (hypothetical alternatives) was originally examined in economic history in a pathbreaking article by John R. Meyer and Alfred H. Conrad, "Economic Theory, Statistical Inference and Economic History," *JEH,* XVII (Dec. 1957). In the literature of philosophy of science, counterfactual propositions have been extensively examined. See Nelson Goodman, "The Problem of Counterfactual Conditions," *JP,* XLIV (Feb. 1947), and R. B. Braithwaite, *Scientific Explanation* (New York : Harper, 1960), pp. 295–318.

better off under a different set of circumstances, fought a revolution, became independent, and changed American history.[7] The actions they pursued were predicated on the views, right or wrong, that they held at that time. Thus, throughout economic history, we are as interested in trying to understand what people thought was happening to them as we are in trying to arrive at an accurate assessment of what actually did happen.[8]

---

[7] Whenever such cases arise, there are two possible explanatory hypotheses : (1) that people were misguided in their economic assessment, or (2) perhaps more plausibly, that they were primarily motivated by other than economic issues.

[8] Since traditional textbooks in history usually carry a full account of what people thought was happening to them, this subject has been slighted in this very brief study except where it necessarily emerges in specific welfare issues, as in Chapters XI and XII.

INSTITUTIONS, PROPERTY RIGHTS, AND ECONOMIC EFFICIENCY

Why aren't all the countries in the world rich? There are few secrets that prevent countries from adopting the latest technology; and if investment in human beings has a big pay off, why don't countries spend more on education and on-the-job training? This question was posed in the last chapter but not answered, because the sources of sustained economic growth and the determinants of income distribution are to be found in the institutional structure of a society. Economic historians can no longer write good economic history without explicitly taking into account—*in theoretical terms*—the institutional structure of the system, both economic and political. We can't avoid the political aspect, because decisions made outside the marketplace have had, and will continue to have, a fundamental influence upon growth and welfare. Nor is it enough to bring in politics *ad hoc*, as historians have done in the past. It must be an integral part of the theory. We are a long way from putting together a comprehensive theory, but we can make a beginning. In this chapter we shall lay out at least the bare bones of an analytical framework, but keep in mind that all the bones in the skeletal framework are not yet in their proper places.

Incentives and economic growth

Societies grow or fail to grow because people act upon or ignore incentives that would lead them to make themselves better off or because the incentives exist or are lacking. Incentives are, obviously, not always material welfare.

The whole history of the Western world, including the settlement of America, illustrates the powerful influence of religious conviction. When we examine the westward movement in the United States we observe people moving west for a variety of reasons—some to escape from monotony, others from debt; some seeking criminal activity, others pursuing adventure; still others, like the Mormons, hoping merely to be left alone. Yet without in any way denying the variety of motives that took people across the Atlantic or the continent, we can make economic sense out of the movements. More people moved when their destinations held promise of potentially high rather than low economic returns. But for the economic system to work in the way we shall describe, it is not necessary that everyone be motivated by economic gain. It is necessary only that a sufficient percentage of the population—often a small minority—be so motivated, in order that a model of economic development based on the assumption of wealth-seeking behavior provide fruitful hypotheses. Current economic analysis and economic history both amply support this proposition, so we can turn to the second and critical element in economic development—the incentives provided by the institutional structure.

The economic system must provide incentives for people to undertake the productive activities described in the previous chapter—that is, it must encourage individuals to innovate, to invest in material and human capital, and so forth. Put more precisely, the private rate of return, the return to the individual, ideally should equal the social rate of return, the net gain that society as a whole receives from the particular economic activity.

Two centuries ago, Adam Smith described how individuals pursuing their own self-interest also improved the well-being of society as a whole. That's another way of saying that private and social rates of return do not greatly differ, although we should note in fairness to Adam Smith that he was concerned about just what kind of institutional structure would produce this result. But why should the two diverge? Private and social rates of return may sometimes be unequal if property rights are incompletely specified or inconsistently enforced. There may then be third-party effects, so that not all the gains and costs associated with an exchange are taken into account by the two parties to an exchange. Somebody else gets into the act. Why should that be so? Let's start with several illustrations from American history and work back to the theory.

Divergence between private and social rates of return

Railroads were constructed across the United States only when the railroad builders viewed the private rate of return as being at least equal to the return on alternative investments. But the gains of society greatly exceeded the gains captured by the railroad builders. The farmer who once was a hundred miles from the nearest railhead suddenly found himself adjacent to cheap transportation; the copper miner who had carried his ore by mule and wagon on a three-day trip to the nearest navigable waterway now had bulk transportation only two hours from his mine; and so on and on. Many people in a variety of activities gained from the availability of the railroad. Note that some of the beneficiaries were parties to the transaction: the farmer and the copper miner gained. But so did anyone who owned land near the right-of-way (whether he shipped on the railroad or not), since his land became much more valuable. The valuable resource was *proximity to the railroad,* over which there were no property rights. Consumers under competitive conditions also benefited from the reduced transport costs that were at least partially passed along in the form of lower prices.

But why didn't the railroad charge each user an amount equal to his gain from the railroad's construction? There may have been a legal prohibition against "discriminatory monopoly" pricing, but a more likely reason is that the costs of measuring and collecting the value of benefits to each user exceeded the gains from making such distinctions. But the implication of the gap between the private and the social rate of return was that the railroad would not necessarily build the road just because in social terms the project was worthwhile. The economic rationale for the whole policy of land grants to railroads was based on raising the private rate of return closer to the social rate, in order to make construction attractive to private builders. We shall explore the issue in a subsequent chapter.

Take another and diametrically opposite example. In the last half of the nineteenth century, manufacturing cities grew up around iron and steel mills that were built near deposits of coal and iron ore in the Ohio Valley. The private rate of return was substantially higher than the social rate because there were significant social costs that the firms did not have to pay. The pollution of water and air was costly, but the costs were not borne by the steel mills; they were paid by the populace, in terms of mortality, sickness, and unpleasant surroundings. Had these additional costs been taken into account (that is, property rights in air and water accurately specified so that they could not be used without compensating those who surrendered their rights to such use) the rate of return to the mills might have been substantially lower. More important, it might then have paid the steel mills to eliminate, or at least to work on eliminating, these undesirable side effects of production. The valuable resource used without compensation in this case was clean air and clean water. No private property rights were defined in these resources; but even if such rights had been defined, enforcing them would probably have been prohibitively expensive, within the enforcement technology of the day.

A final example comes from our early history. In the seventeenth and eighteenth centuries, ocean trade was beset by pirates and privateers who plundered ships and their goods. The enforcement of property rights was frequently in the hands of the individual shipper, who had to incur the heavy costs of arming and manning his ships with trained gunners. The costs to both the shipper and the ultimate buyer were therefore raised. One solution was to arm ships; another was to convoy them; a third solution, used by the British in the Mediterranean, was to bribe the pirates to leave British ships alone; and a fourth solution was to destroy them, which the young American Republic tried on one occasion (against the Barbary pirates in the early 1800s). The choice of solution depended upon the perceived relative costs and benefits of each. In this case, the problem was the enforcement of a well-defined property right.

Property rights and efficiency

These illustrations reflect either the absence of well-defined property rights to valuable resources or a lack of enforcement. The problems persist because: (1) We may not have the technical knowledge to exclude third parties from benefiting or from incurring some of the costs. In all the third-party illustrations above, deficient technical knowledge made measurement too expensive: eliminating the effects was not worthwhile. (2) The organizational costs of bringing together the concerned third parties (dependent at least in part on the state of technology) may exceed the potential gains. This reason, too, was evident in all the above instances.

Transaction costs are the costs of maintaining and exchanging private property rights over resource use. In the absence of transaction costs, the problems of achieving growth (assuming that the members of society desire a rising per capita income) are simple. We can see this clearly by applying it to the two key elements in promoting growth: technological change and investment in human capital, which we discussed in the previous chapter.

If an inventor or innovator received all the gains from the development and application of new knowledge (i.e., if the private and social rates of return were equal) then the incentive to develop new technology would be much greater than they are. But if an inventor spends years developing a superior machine, only to see it pirated and used by others without compensation to him, then he will receive only a very small fraction of the social benefits, and the costs of years of research may well exceed these benefits. In order to encourage invention and innovation, we need institutional arrangements that will specify and enforce property rights in new ideas and their application to economic activity. One solution is patent laws, which attempt to give the inventor monopoly rights for a number of years; but even here the costs of enforcement make this a very imperfect solution, as Eli Whitney found out with the cotton gin. He devoted years of his life to litigation against those who appropriated his invention without compensation.

Similarly, if the returns to society of a better educated populace exceed the gains that the individual gets from more schooling and training, then it may not be worth his while to pay the costs of additional education, since the benefits to him may be less than the costs. While the society may gain from better educated people who are less prone to crime, delinquency, etc., there is no direct property right which will give these gains to the student. One solution is to have the state subsidize education.

The study of economic growth must therefore focus on those institutional arrangements that enable individuals and groups to be more productive by realizing economies of scale (the corporation), encourage innovation (prizes, patent laws), improve the efficiency of capital markets (banks, bills of exchange), or reduce market imperfections (insurance companies, futures markets). Some institutional arrangements can be created without changing property rights, simply by developing (innovating) new organizational forms of voluntary organization (many forms of business organization such as stock markets and commodity markets required no legal change for this innovation); others require new legal backing (general incorporation laws), and still others are directly created by government.

Whatever type of new institutional arrangement is devised, it involves real costs; and the private benefits must exceed the costs, to make it worthwhile. Several consequences are immediately evident. (1) The social benefits of forming new institutional arrangements may be substantially higher than the private benefits, since, as noted above, devising property rights in ideas has been, and continues to be, difficult and costly. (2) Costs associated with forming voluntary institutions are different from those connected with governmental ones. If I form a partnership but subsequently don't like the policies that the other partners persist in, I can withdraw from that partnership and form a new business. But if I join with others in getting my political representatives to pass a zoning ordinance restricting the use of property and subsequently do not like this result, I cannot simply withdraw from obeying the zoning ordinance. I am stuck with the result. I can always move away, of course, but the costs of withdrawal are much higher than in the partnership.

The role of government

This brings us to the role of government. As a first approximation, we can view government as an institutional arrangement formed by the citizens to undertake the protection and enforcement of property rights. But why shouldn't everyone protect his own property rights (just as the early shipper did by arming his ships)? The answer is that there are economies of scale in protection and enforcement of property rights, so that they can be done much more cheaply by a central coercive body than by each voluntary group. That is, protection is a *semipublic good*, by which we mean that it costs no more to protect the property of two persons than it does to protect the property of one.[1] And therein lies the first problem. While everyone wants his property rights protected, he has an incentive to enjoy a free ride and let the other fellow pay for the protection. The obvious solution is

---

[1] If it were a *pure public good*, we could protect an infinite number of people at no additional cost; but clearly beyond some point costs rise.

that the citizens give the government the coercive power to tax everyone for the service.

Typically, when governments are formed, they set out a basic set of rules, the fundamental institutional arrangements. In the United States this was done by the Constitutional Convention of 1787, and we shall examine the consequences in more detail in Chapter V. These fundamental institutions serve to reduce uncertainty. In their complete absence, chaos would reign. They tell us what to expect, and we can act accordingly. Secondary institutional arrangements are made within the context (at least nominally) of these basic rules.

It's obvious that the government's role in protecting property rights is a necessary prerequisite to economic growth in a market economy. But it is equally demonstrable that government can be blamed when economic growth fails to take place. First, we must define just what the state is. In early modern times it was reasonable to view the state as something akin to a firm that specialized in selling protection and justice. There were many competitiors (feudal lords who aspired to greater roles) willing to provide these services at a price. In such an environment the state was something apart from the members of the political unit. We also observe that where successful economic growth occurred, representative bodies wrested power away from monarchs in return for revenue. By the end of the seventeenth century in English parliamentary government, a more or less representative body of the citizenry dominated nonmarket decision making, and in a real sense the state was not independent of its constituents (as was Louis XIV for example). Both in the independent (and even absolute) monarchy and in the representative state, the relationship between subjects and the state was a contractual one; but in the representative government, the individuals who made up the state were elected.

Market and nonmarket decision making

Economists are fond of comparing the market decision-making process with that of political democracy. In the first instance the consumer influences decisions by how he spends his income. His changing income and tastes lead to the rise and fall of firms and industries and therefore guide the changes that take place. In fact, economic growth as described in Chapter I comes about automatically, given that the behavioral assumptions described above are valid and assuming that government does nothing more than specify and enforce private property rights over all valuable resources. But clearly, nonmarket decision making is not parallel to choice in the market, and we simply cannot stick with the first approximation that we made in discussing government. Historically we observe that it is quite likely that government —including representative government—will devise property rights (both by legislative and by judicial action) that hamper growth or even prevent it altogether. We have the evidence all around us in the contemporary underdeveloped world as well as in the historically different growth experience of countries around the world. How can we account for these differences in the pattern of governmental involvement?

A satisfactory theory of the state is far from a reality, but we can—and indeed must if we are to make major advances in economic history—make a start. Although the following points by no means add up to a theory of the state, they strongly suggest why nonmarket decision making is very different from choice in the marketplace, and they illuminate why governmental actions need not produce a more efficient economic system. Let us compare the consumer and the producer.

(1) A consumer who wants to buy a product—a stove for example —in the marketplace can directly purchase it. In contrast, if he wishes to buy more of a service—say, crime protection—in the political system, he cannot buy it directly; he can only vote for the candidate he believes most likely to devote the desired fiscal resources to crime prevention. While the consumer in the market knows he is going to get the stove, the voter has only one vote among many and therefore does not know the outcome.

(2)This leads us to information costs. Information is never really free. It costs search time (which is time forgone from other activities) and sometimes requires direct money outlays for the purchase of informational material. But the consumer buying the stove has much more incentive to seek information about the desired product (since he knows he is going to buy one) than does any "political purchaser," since the likelihood that his vote will make any difference is negligible. In fact, unless he believes that the prospective election may be close, he has little incentive to vote at all.[2]

---

[2] See Yoram Barzel and Gene Silberberg, "Is the Act of Voting Rational?" *Public Choice,* Spring 1973.

(3) The consumer buys a single product—a stove—but the voter votes for a package of promises, since the office seekers run on a whole platform of issues. This raises still further the costs of information necessary to know what the voter is voting for. Ideologies are substitutes for search costs—we buy a radical, liberal, conservative, or reactionary candidate rather than invest in the costs of really finding out about each issue (assuming that we bother to vote at all).

Let's turn to the producer side:

(1) A firm tries to maximize profits and competes with other firms by means of price, quality, and advertising. The office seeker tries to put together and advertise the package of promises that will get him the greatest number of votes.[3]

(2) A firm borrows funds from a financial institution on the promise of repayment with interest or a share of the profits. An office seeker receives campaign contributions from those who believe that he will further their interests. Individuals and groups with a big stake in the political outcome will be willing to invest heavily because the potential returns are great. For example, the mafia will find it worthwhile to invest heavily in a candidate who (despite his campagn promises) will go easy on crime. Similar reasoning applies to public school teachers, firms subject to government regulation, and trade unions subject to governmental action. In general we are simply making the familiar point that government favors producer groups over consumers.

(3) To the firm, one consumer is like another. To the political representative this is not true. Voters who feel strongly about a single issue and will judge a candidate on that issue alone, even though a minority of voters, are much more influential than the rest of the voters, who feel less strongly about any single issue and will scatter their votes accordingly.

(4) The most striking contrast of all is the measurement of performance. Large-scale private and governmental organizations nurture the growth of bureaucracy, and the relationship of bureaucracy to the measurement of performance becomes more attenuated, the further it is removed from competitive conditions. In a competitive industry, a relatively inefficient bureaucracy would go bankrupt. How-

---

[3] Note that this is not necessarily only a bare majority of the votes, since a landslide victory will scare off future candidates and give him more influence in the legislature.

ever, no such constraint limits the growth of a nonmarket bureaucracy (where substantial monopoly power exists, this result may occur even in a market).

While the preceding characteristics of market and nonmarket decision making neither exhaust their differences nor put them into a coherent model, they do enable us to see why government activity will not necessarily increase economic efficiency. The government has the coercive power to limit entry into an industry and create monopoly, to hinder factor mobility, to thwart innovation. But why would it pursue such policies when more efficient property rights would increase total output and income? Surely if there were some who suffered from more efficient property rights, the gainers could compensate the losers and still be better off, since total income has increased. However, when transaction costs are taken into account, it may not be worthwhile to compensate the losers. We have also noted that the protection and enforcement of property rights are semipublic goods, so that as the size of the market grows it does become worthwhile to devise new and more efficient institutional arrangements. With basic rules (i.e., a constitution) that make it very costly for legislators to do otherwise, this may indeed be the outcome (we shall explore this idea in much more detail in Chapter V). But it is equally possible to have basic rules that make redistribution of income via monopoly (broadly conceived to cover both product and factor markets) a more profitable activity. The reasons parallel those for the market. Some groups benefit more than others in relation to the costs of their political activity. Take the case of the mill towns of the Ohio Valley. Each inhabitant suffered from poorer health and filthy surroundings as a result of the steel mills' pollution, but it would be extremely expensive for them to organize and demand compensation for the mill or—even better—to elect legislators who would tax the polluters. Each inhabitant, therefore, preferred to let others pay the organizing costs. On the other hand, the steel mill owners had a direct and big stake in supporting the campaigns of legislative candidates who (whatever their public promises) would prevent the enactment of antipollution legislation.

Historical changes in the relative profitability of employing the political process to provide more efficient property rights, or to provide property rights that lower efficiency or whose aim is income redistribution will be a focal point of much of our subsequent analysis.

Before we conclude this chapter, one important caveat should be issued. This book does not make the normative judgment that increased efficiency is good, but income redistribution is bad. Indeed, in the concluding chapters we shall see that a majority of the society may choose quite freely to give up some degree of efficiency in exchange for other values and may consciously vote (with varying degrees of success) to redistribute income from the rich to the poor. The object of the book is to provide as scientific a framework of analysis as possible to explain growth and welfare in the American past, not to make judgments.

AN OVERVIEW OF
THE DEVELOPMENT
OF THE U.S. ECONOMY

Before examining specific issues of growth and welfare, we need an overview of the growth and structural changes of the past three and one-half centuries. The topography of this economic landscape can be seen in the following tables and charts drawn from the accumulation of statistical data. They are supplemented at many points by the rich accumulation of qualitative information gathered from the literature of economic history.

The growth rate

Since the earliest national income estimate of 1840, the economy has grown at a rate about 1.6 percent per year in real terms (Fig.III·1). This means that in terms of constant prices, the average per capita income has risen 1.6 percent, and this is roughly analogous to what has actually happened to the average standard of life or the average well-being of people, although we must remember the caution in the first chapter that there are limitations to using per capita income figures and drawing too neat a pattern from them. At first glance, 1.6 percent may not sound like a very impressive annual growth rate, but it turns out to have quite spectacular compound results. It means that every 43 years, income per capita, in constant prices, has doubled in America. In today's prices, average income per head exceeds $4,000, whereas back in 1840 when measurements began, it was less than one tenth that figure in today's prices. This raises the question: what happened before 1840? We lack information on income before that

Fig. III · 1   PER CAPITA INCOME, 1840–1940

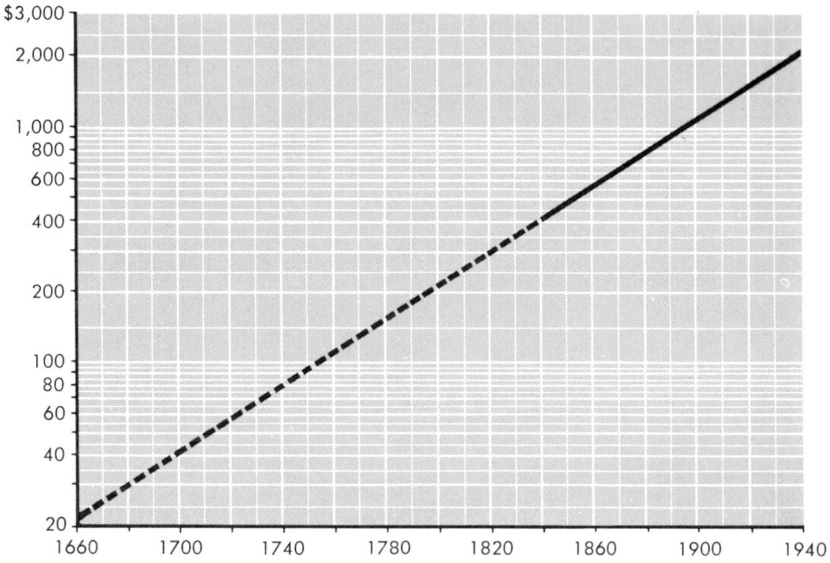

Source : Raymond Goldsmith, testimony before the U.S. Cong. *JEC*, printed in "Employment, Growth, and the Price Level," 86th Cong, 1st Sess., Part II, 1959 (Washington : GPO, 1959), pp. 277–78.

date. Less is known about the economy, and the statistics are still far from adequate. It is probable, however, that per capita real income grew at a slower pace.

Figure III · 1 illustrates why the growth rate of 1.6 percent per year probably did not exist much earlier than 1840. Projected back before that date, the same growth rate very rapidly reaches unreasonably low levels of per capita income. The extended line indicates that in today's dollars, per capita annual income would have been $145 in 1776; $80 in 1740, and $30 in 1680. Since the early Americans did not starve, these are ridiculous figures, having no real significance. It therefore appears likely that the rate of growth of the economy must have been slower in the period before 1840 (although when the change takes place, we don't know). This point has some significance for later analysis.

The colonial era

What were of the salient features of the colonial economy? First of all, 90 percent of the people farmed or worked in related pursuits.

However, there was little increase in the productivity of farming in the colonial period, and therefore little growth in per capita income resulting from productivity gains in agriculture. Some improvements in efficiency did occur with increases in the size of the market and with better marketing methods; however, there was comparatively little shift to better land during this period, and it is doubtful that living standards rose rapidly.

Meanwhile, really substantial gains in productivity were taking place in another part of our economy that was another main source of income—international shipping. In colonial times, America was already a major shipping power, engaging in fishing, whaling, and particularly in carrying the goods of the world—not only from our own shores to other nations, but between foreign countries. Colonial productivity in shipping improved substantially during that period and became an important feature of the total economy. A good share of credit for the increased productivity goes to an event seldom thought of today—the decline in piracy. As freebooters were driven from the seas, fewer men and guns were needed for protection on ships, and this saving turned out to be an important source of lowering the real cost of ocean transportation.

In colonial times there was little manufacturing. Shipbuilding was an important activity, and there were some small-scale manufacturing activities like making iron. By and large, however, it was a farming, shipping, and commercial society, not heavily involved in manufacturing. Since America of that day was a small market with relatively expensive labor, it is not surprising that the English provided most of our manufacturing.

In terms of the determinants of economic growth discussed in Chapter I, the colonial economy would be expected to improve only gradually and probably not at the 1.6 percent per year figure cited for more recent times. There was little technological change in agriculture, the major source of income. And improvements that were occurring in economic organization were still very gradual, in the forms of increasing productivity in shipping, of larger markets, of the beginnings of towns, and of better communication and transportation. It is doubtful, therefore, that the colonial economy could have been expected to grow as strikingly overall as it did after 1840.

What about the *extensive* growth of the colonial period? Rapid population growth certainly characterized the period. A glance at Fig. III·2 gives an approximation of the course of colonial population,

Fig. III · 2   POPULATION OF AMERICAN COLONIES, 1610–1780

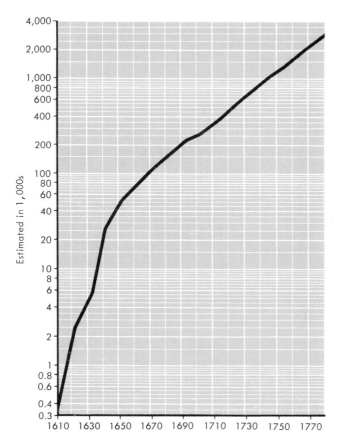

Source: *Hist. Statistics* (Washington: GPO, 1960), Ser. Z 1–19, p. 756.

increasing from negligible numbers up to 331,000 by 1710, then soaring to more than 2,000,000 at the time of the Revolutionary War. Immigrants made up some of this increase. Many came voluntarily, free and clear; others put themselves into indenture, agreeing to work for someone for a prescribed period in return for payment of their passage and for specified benefits at the end of the indenture. Still others, in substantial numbers, were brought in as slaves who provided a great share of the labor force in the southern colonies. Extensive growth in the colonial period, therefore, consisted of a notable increase of population; settlements along the coasts, a gradual movement into the interior, and the beginning of an economy based upon agriculture and shipping, which will be examined further on in more detail.

Colonial days were turbulent. The settlers frequently had grievances against the British, against the French and Spanish on their borders, against the Indians along the frontier, and at times against each other. These disputes reflected the colonists' views that their welfare was being adversely affected, and at times they led to open warfare. The actual income effects of these controversies have not been measured. The most significant for American history were the issues between the Crown and the colonists from 1763 to 1775, which are examined in the following chapter.

The nineteenth century

Turning now to the nineteenth century (beginning, however, with the first census, which was in 1790), we may take a sweeping look at the pattern of that century's economy. Table III·1 points up agriculture's predominant role in commodity output. In 1839, when figures were first obtained, agriculture accounted for 70 percent of the value added. Certain agricultural commodities were particularly important. Of these, cotton played a dominant early role and was a large part of total

TABLE III·1	VALUE ADDED BY INDUSTRY IN CURRENT PRICES, 1839–1899 (in billions of dollars)			
Year ▼	Total ▼	Agriculture ▼	Mining ▼	Manufacturing ▼	Construction ▼
1839	$ 1.04	$0.71	$0.01	$0.24	$0.08
1844	1.09	0.69	0.01	0.31	0.08
1849	1.40	0.83	0.02	0.45	0.11
1854	2.39	1.46	0.03	0.66	0.23
1859	2.57	1.50	0.03	0.82	0.23
1869	4.83	2.54	0.13	1.63	0.54
1874	5.40	2.53	0.15	2.07	0.65
1879	5.30	2.60	0.15	1.96	0.59
1884	7.09	2.84	0.20	3.05	1.01
1889	7.87	2.77	0.28	3.73	1.10
1894	7.83	2.64	0.29	3.60	1.30
1899	10.20	3.40	0.47	5.04	1.29

Source: *Hist. Statistics*, Ser. F 10–21, p. 139.

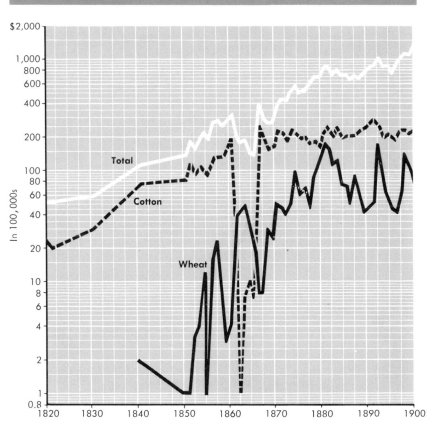

Fig. III · 3 **TOTAL EXPORTS AND WHEAT AND COTTON EXPORTS, 1820-1900**

Source: *Hist. Statistics* (Washington: GPO, 1960), Ser. U 61–72, pp. 546–47.

exports. As Fig. III·3 shows, cotton comprised more than half of American exports in the years before the Civil War. After the war, it continued as an important part of the agricultural economy, although the value of wheat exports became a significant and growing challenger.

Agriculture expanded with the opening and settlement of the West. It is not surprising, therefore, that as new, rich lands were developed, the agricultural output continually expanded and the kinds of agriculture became diversified. A second look at Table III·1 shows another noteworthy development. Although agriculture grew all

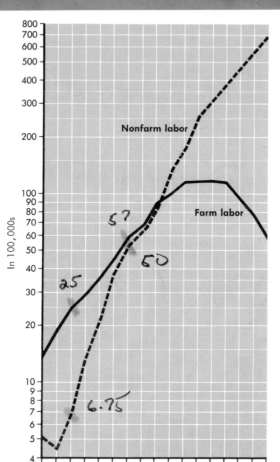

Fig. III · 4   FARM AND NONFARM LABOR FORCE, 1800–1960

Source: Stanley Lebergott, "Labor Force and Employment, 1800–1960," *Output, Employment, and Productivity in the United States after 1800* (New York: National Bureau of Economic Research, 1966), p. 118.

through the century in absolute terms of value added, *relatively* it declined. It was 70 per cent of commodity output in 1839 and only 33 percent of output by the end of that century. Different statistics illustrate the same point in Fig. III·4, which shows the composition of the labor force during the century. How were people employed? Two million out of 2.8 million people worked on the land, and other aspects of the economy were relatively negligible. As the century moved forward, however, the change in the employment pattern became striking. It is true that the number of agricultural workers increased; but growing much more rapidly were the tallies of those working in manufacturing, construction, transportation, and trade. Later in the century, proportionately more and more were working in activities other than agriculture; as a matter of fact, 1910 was a peak year in absolute terms for agricultural workers, whose total has been declining ever since that date. The distribution of the labor force reveals impressively that while we were a rapidly growing agricultural economy, other sectors—particularly manufacturing—were growing even more rapidly. By 1880, only half our people worked in agriculture.

When people shift from agriculture to other activities, comparable shifts are expected in how they live. They will move off the farms to the cities, and that is what shows up in Fig. III·5, which classifies "urban" as communities of 2,500 or more, and "rural" as com-

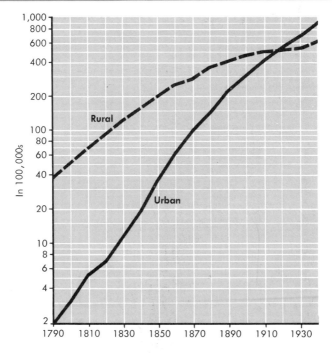

Fig. III · 5 POPULATION IN URBAN AND RURAL TERRITORY, BY SIZE OF PLACE, 1790–1940

Source: *Hist. Statistics* (Washington: GPO, 1960), Ser. A 195–209, p. 14.

munities of less than that number. The distribution is continually moving in the direction of an increasingly urban society. By the twentieth century, America was becoming predominantly urban, but not until 1920 did urban territory include more people than did rural territory. The whole process of westward movement and shift from farm to city is tied to where people worked and the kinds of jobs they had. A side-light to this pattern of rural-urban relationship is evident in Fig. III·6, which shows the birth rate in America. The decline from 52 per thousand in 1820 to approximately 22 per thousand in 1960 (and 18 per thousand in the present decade) was first of all related to the shift from farm to cities. Children used to be much more of an asset on the farm and less costly to raise than in the city. Today, farm birth rates are close to those for urban areas, generally mirroring the fact that children are becoming relatively more costly in both city and country.

Fig. III · 6   ANNUAL BIRTH RATE AND TREND, 1820–1960

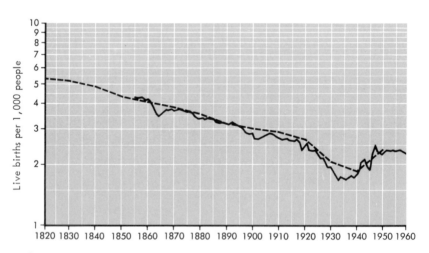

Source: Ansley J. Coale and Melvin Zelnik, *New Estimates of Fertility and Population in the United, States* (Princeton, N.J.: Princeton Univ., 1963); yearly estimates, *Hist. Statistics*, p. 23.

An integral part of nineteenth-century expansion was the growth of our banking system, of wholesale and retail marketing organization, and a more efficient transportation network. All contributed significantly to productivity increase by lowering the real costs of credit and of handling and moving goods.

The high cost of carrying bulk goods in colonial times limited commercial production to areas adjacent to navigable waterways. Improved roads and then turnpikes after the Revolutionary War widened local markets, but the major improvements in internal transportation came with the growth of water transport on the Mississippi River system (particularly with the innovation of the steamboat for upriver carriage of goods in 1816) and the growth of a canal system connecting the Great Lakes with both the Mississippi system and with the eastern seaboard. The development of the railroad after 1830, in turn, displaced the canal and dominated internal transport history (Chapter IX).

The orientation of the colonies toward external markets (and the purchase of goods from abroad) led to rather well-developed merchant houses dealing in exports and imports; however, as internal trade and commerce grew, institutions to move goods from producers to consumers also grew and necessarily became more complex. The evolution from itinerant peddler, jobber, roving merchant, and general store (often associated with a local factory) to specialized wholesale houses and equally specialized retail outlets was a nineteenth-century development, and it is mirrored in the growing percentage of the labor force engaged in trade, increasing from about 6 percent in 1850 to more than 10 percent by the turn of the century.

Banking was in its infancy the decade after independence was achieved. The first chartered bank was established in 1784, but banking growth was slow in early years. The establishment of the first United States Bank in 1791 provided an important impetus for tying together government fiscal activities with the early banking community. Although the bank was an important step in the growth of the capital market, it engendered considerable opposition, and its charter was not renewed after its initial twenty-year term. Five years later, however, in 1816, the second United States Bank was chartered. After a rocky start under undistinguished leadership it became, under Nicholas Biddle, a major influence in regulating commercial banks, in acting as a reserve bank when banks needed additional specie, and in integrating the banking system. In short, it anticipated in many respects the role expected of a modern central bank in influencing the money supply and tying together federal government fiscal activities with the banking system. It became an even more controversial institution than its predecessor, and it was a central issue in the election of 1832. When Andrew Jackson triumphed, the bank's fate was settled; and with the expiration of its charter, central banking was not again to be revived until the next century.

The demise of the second bank resulted in a mounting number of banks, each issuing its own notes. By 1860 there were 1,500 banks individually issuing, on the average, six different types of notes. Moreover, the worth of the notes varied strikingly—some were "as good as gold," others were the worthless paper of broken banks. The Civil War and growing pressure for a national banking system led to the passage in 1864 of the National Banking Act, which permitted federal charter of banks and required that such banks keep reserves in cash or as deposits with a national bank in one of seventeen large cities. Similarly, banks in these large cities had the same option to keep part of their reserves in New York City banks. The result was the beginning of a nationwide banking system. A central banking system to unite federal government fiscal policy with the banking system did not occur, however, until the creation of the Federal Reserve System in 1914.

One more aspect, important to the economy in the nineteenth century (and particularly in its first half) was our relationship with the rest of the world. We were but a small part of the great world, and the fact that foreigners wanted our goods and services contributed significantly to our extensive expansion. Cotton and shipping have already been discussed. But foreigners also wanted other kinds of goods—agricultural products in the early part of the nineteenth century and then, as the century wore on and we became an industrial nation, our manufactured goods as well.

Perhaps more important than the role of trade in the country's growth was immigration. Figure III·7 pictures this immensely significant aspect of our overall development. Beginning in the 1840s with the Irish famine and its consequences, vast numbers of people turned to America in a tide that flowed through the decades until World War I. This was a swelling movement of unprecedented numbers willing to take their chances in a New World. Undoubtedly, it was one of the important formative aspects of our expansion.

Foreigners also invested heavily in the new nation, as illustrated

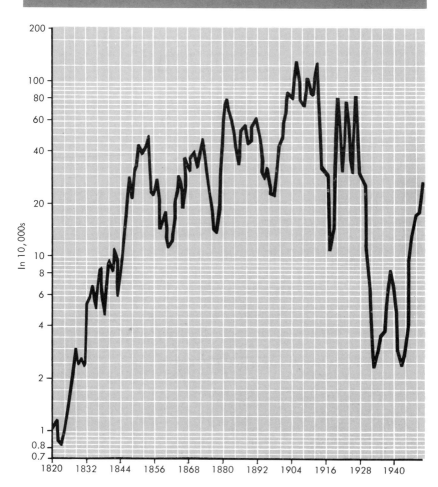

Fig. III · 7   IMMIGRATION, 1820–1950

Source: *Hist. Statistics* (Washington: GPO, 1960), Ser. C 133–38, p. 62.

in Fig. III·8. The British particularly, having confidence in America's future, invested in canals, railroads, and cotton plantations. Although foreign investment was significant, it probably has been overstressed in the history of national development. Foreign capital was important in the 1830's, but thereafter its proportion of total capital formation dwindled, even though the absolute amount grew substantially.

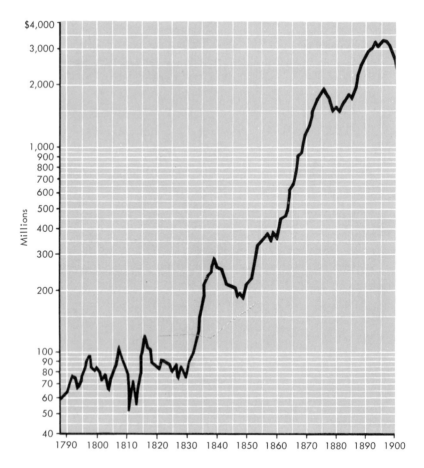

**Fig. III · 8   FOREIGN INVESTMENT IN U.S.
(NET LIABILITIES) 1789–1900**

Source: *Hist. Statistics* (Washington: GPO, 1960), Ser. U 207, p. 566.

Overall, the international economy contributed through investment; it contributed through people; and it contributed through trade —we bought goods that could be produced less expensively elsewhere and sold goods that we could produce relatively inexpensively. It also contributed in one essential way that cannot be shown in graphic form —ideas. The technology America borrowed in the nineteenth century, basically from Europe and particularly from Great Britain, was a major source of improvement in productivity.

By 1860 the United States had become a major industrial nation, second only to Britain. Figure III·9 shows the decade rate of growth in commodity output. The progress of America into first place among

Fig. III · 9   COMMODITY OUTPUT IN 5-YEAR AVERAGES, 1839–1899

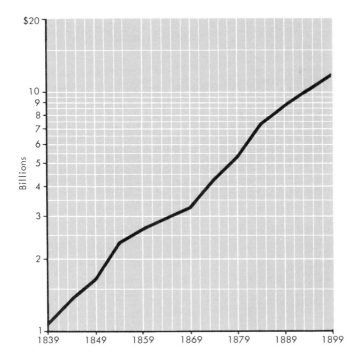

Source: Robert E. Gallman, "The United States Commodity Output, 1839–1899," *Trends in the American Economy in the Nineteenth Century,* a report of the NBER (Princeton, N.J.: Princeton Univ., 1960), pp. 16, 43.

industrial nations may be seen in Table III·2, showing the percentages of world manufacturing output from 1870 to 1929. From 23 percent in 1870, the nation's share rose to more than 40 percent of the world's manufacturing output by 1926–1929. Between the Civil War and World War I, an already thriving manufacturing enormously expanded.

TABLE III·2   U.S. PERCENTAGE OF WORLD MANUFACTURING OUTPUT (world = 100 percent)

Period ▼	U.S.A. ▼	United Kingdom ▼	Germany ▼	France ▼	Russia ▼	Others ▼
1870	23.3	31.8	13.2	10.3	3.7	17.7
1881–1885	28.6	26.6	13.9	8.6	3.4	18.9
1896–1900	30.1	19.5	16.6	7.1	5.0	21.7
1906–1910	35.3	14.7	15.9	6.4	5.0	22.7
1913	35.8	14.0	15.7	6.4	5.5	22.6
1926–1929	42.2	9.4	11.6	6.6	4.3	25.9

Source: League of Nations, *Industrialization and Foreign Trade* (Geneva, 1945), p. 13.

TABLE III·3   POPULATION REDISTRIBUTION (percent of total)

Region ▼	1870 ▼	1880 ▼	1890 ▼	1900 ▼
New England	8.8	8.0	7.5	7.4
Middle Atlantic	24.7	23.4	22.5	22.5
Great Lakes	22.9	22.3	21.4	21.0
Southeast	29.1	27.3	25.5	25.1
Plains	9.7	12.3	14.2	13.6
Southwest	2.5	3.5	4.4	5.5
Mountain	0.4	0.9	1.4	1.7
Far West	1.8	2.3	3.1	3.2
U.S. total	39,818,449	50,155,783	62,947,714	75,994,575

Source: Original from 17th U.S. Census, 1950, as contained in Harvey S. Perloff, *et al., Regions,*

At the same time, population was redistributing itself around the United States. In the early days, of course, all settlement was along the eastern coastal line; by 1860, the population was moving out across the Appalachian Mountains into the Great Lakes area, the Middle Atlantic area, and into the cotton-producing South. The Gold Rush of 1848 pushed the frontiers of population westward to California and Oregon. After the Civil War, the movement was primarily across the Mississippi into the rich area of the plains, that whole vast area from the Mississippi to the Rocky Mountains, which became settled during that period. Population expanded from New England, the oldest area, into the Midwest and then into the Far West. This particular pattern, taking place all through that period, is traced in Table III·3, as it occurred from 1870 on. Not only were people relocating, but they were continually moving into new and rich agricultural lands. At the same time that America rose to first place among manufacturing nations of the world, it also became the world's leading agricultural nation. In short, America became a supplier to the world both of industrial products and of greatly increased output of agricultural products.

The nineteenth century, therefore, was marked not only by an unprecedented increase in people, capital, and land—spurring its extensive growth—but also by increasing productivity of these production factors, resulting in intensive growth. The most noteworthy aspects were (1) adoption of the most productive techniques in the world in

1910 ▼	1920 ▼	1930 ▼	1940 ▼	1950 ▼
7.1	7.0	6.7	6.4	6.2
23.0	23.1	23.3	23.0	22.3
19.8	20.3	20.6	20.2	20.2
23.9	23.0	22.2	22.9	22.4
12.7	11.9	10.8	10.8	9.3
6.6	7.0	7.4	7.4	7.6
2.2	2.4	2.2	2.3	2.3
4.7	5.3	6.8	7.5	9.7
91,972,266	105,710,620	122,775,046	131,669,275	150,697,361

Resources, and Economic Growth (Baltimore: Johns Hopkins Univ., 1960), pp. 124, 225.

manufacturing and in agriculture; (2) significant increase in education in America, making possible the use of the latest technology and a new productivity stemming from substantial research both in industry and in agriculture; and (3) availability of a vast new United States market of unprecedented size, which made feasible all the advantages of large-scale production.

If overall growth characterized this period, so did frequently recurring economic distress and hardship for diverse groups. The most important sources of such distress were the recurrent depressions and recessions of the nineteenth century; 1819, 1837, 1839, 1857, 1873, and 1893 were all years that marked the onset of falling income and increasing unemployment of varying degress of severity. There are not accurate statistics to measure the fall in income or the amount of unemployment during these periods. As an increasing percentage of the population shifted from self-sufficient agriculture to production for the market, the impact of these depressions became greater, since they affected more and more people.

The immigrant or the farm boy who left the farm was likely to seek employment in the new factory towns as manufacturing grew. His hours were long and the conditions onerous by present standards. Factory towns were frequently unsanitary, overlaid with coal dust; housing conditions were grim. Although it is doubtful that the new factory worker's real income fell (Chapter VI), he bore the serious costs of monotonous discipline during long hours at a machine and the insecurity of employment, as workers were let out during depressions.

The farmer's well-being, too, was becoming more dependent upon the market. On top of drought, locusts, and other natural disasters, wide fluctuations in prices received for crops made his income subject to broad swings (Chapter XI). His lot improved in the nineteenth century, but this undeniable statement hides the diversity of economic experience that held disaster in the short run for many.

It is not surprising, therefore, that the nineteenth century was characterized by a variety of protest movements against working conditions, job insecurity, low prices, and monopoly.

Utopian schemes and programs of reform were continually advanced as solutions to these problems. Trade-union membership was never a significant percentage of the labor force until well into the twentieth century. Attempts to form a nationwide labor organization such as the National Labor Union in 1866 and the Knights of Labor (which had its major expansion in the 1870s and early 1880s) turned out to be temporary, and it was not until the founding of the American Federation of Labor in 1886 that trade unions achieved permanent organization on a national basis. Farm protest movements had a larger impact upon public policy. Between the Civil War and 1900, the Greenback, Granger, and Populist movements attempted to increase prices and to undertake basic economic reforms in the expectation that they would raise farm real income (Chapter XI). We know very little about the distribution of income in the nineteenth century. It certainly was unequal but probably not nearly as unequal as it was in Europe.

A source of mounting concern to worker and farmer was the development of the trust and of other forms of organization having significant monopoly power. Henry Demarest Lloyd's *Wealth Against Commonwealth* and Ida Tarbell's *History of the Standard Oil Company* provided early examples of the proliferating literature of reformers and muckrakers protesting against the growth of monopoly. The reformers not only pointed up the dangers of the trust but exposed political graft and corruption and tried to make Americans aware of the importance of conserving and setting aside the rich natural-resource heritage of forests and scenic attractions in the face of the onrushing extensive expansion of the economy.

The twentieth century

World War I marks the end of an era, a boundary beyond which nations became more self-contained. America dammed the stream of immigration, and other countries erected tariff barriers, as we had done earlier. An international economy in which people, capital, and ideas had enjoyed free interchanges for a century became hampered by restrictions on the movement of people and by restrictions on trade. World War I also marked the end of a relatively peaceful century and the beginning of a century marked by global war and a global depression. The decade of the Twenties was prosperous, but the 1929 crash and subsequent decade of depression resulted in a greater fall in income and a more cataclysmic economic period than any ever experienced before. It had long-run implications for our future views about how to cope with comparable situations and about the policies to be pursued. The depression of the Thirties continued in some measure until our 1941 entry into World War II and the resultant explosive expansion to meet war needs.

In taking this overview of what happened in the twentieth century—a notable growth of the economy interrupted by the Great Depression but continued thereafter—a few salient changes should be recognized. One was the development of new products. The twentieth century introduced the automobile, the electric refrigerator, and all the other comforts known as durable consumer goods; and it witnessed a vast demand for services, compared with goods. The result was a significant change in the employment pattern and in the structure of the economy to meet these new demands of a prospering people.[1] A second change was a turnabout in America's international role: instead of being a debtor nation, as it was at the turn of the century, it became a creditor; and since World War II, it has expended vast sums attempting to promote and assist the development of the rest of the world. It has also expended vast sums in controversial wars that divided the nation. And a third transformation was one that took place in the role of government in the American economy. When the federal government first emerged in 1790, it spent but a tiny fraction of national income and was involved in relatively few concerns. Contrast the role of government in the American economy today! The federal government alone (forgetting for the moment state and local governments) has an annual budget in the neighborhood of $200 billion. Government at all levels expends somewhere around a quarter of total national income. Obviously, government now has a role different from any it has ever had before—one of vastly more scope in regulating and ordering the working of our economy (Chapter XIV).

This brief sketch of American economic experience will serve as a backdrop for an analytical explanation of specific issues of growth and welfare. We begin with colonial America.

---

[1] Between 1919 and 1957, while nonagricultural employment doubled, employment in services tripled. *Hist. Statistics* (Washington: GPO, 1960), p. 73.

EUROPEAN EXPANSION AND COLONIAL DEVELOPMENT

Colonial settlement was a direct outgrowth of the expansion of western Europe in the fifteenth, sixteenth, and seventeenth centuries. The Western world was emerging from a relatively self-sufficient feudal society in which people produced most of their own goods, raised their own food, made their own clothing and equipment. It had been a world in which trade and commerce played a relatively minor role, a world characterized in western Europe by the self-contained economy of the manor house and the small village that the manor house dominated. Now this picture was changing.

The European background

The conditions that had given rise to the feudal world were a lack of order, scarce labor, abundant land, and differential military endowments. In this context serfs and free men provided labor services in return for the protection and justice (embodied in the custom of the manor) provided by the lord. Population, which apparently declined in the chaotic conditions that followed the collapse of the Roman Empire, now began to grow again. But the lands around the manor could support only so many laborers before local returns to labor diminished rapidly; additional laborers had to work poorer land, and their output was less than that of their predecessors. Over the whole of Europe, however, this was no problem, because there were vast empty parts of the Continent still to be settled. We are used to thinking of the frontier movement as being associated with the nineteenth-century American West, but it is well to remember that our frontier was only a continuation of a movement that began (or to be more exact, was revived) as early as the tenth century.

The spread of settlement throughout western Europe provided increased inducements for trade. The resource endowments of settled areas were increasingly diverse, with varying soils, climates, and topography. The cool, moist climate of England produced excellent wool; the soil and climate of Bordeaux yielded fine wine grapes; and so forth. Moreover, concentrated population centers provided different skills; that is, investment in human capital varied from place to place. All this added up to growing opportunities for trade. Furthermore, the filling out of Europe's wilderness had reduced the area of brigands, and there was a growing incentive to protect long distance trade. The resultant development of an exchange economy, together with the increasing scarcity of good land as population expanded, basically altered the conditions that had made feudalism a viable system. As land became scarcer, its potential value increased; but as long as exclusive private ownership did not exist, no one could capture these potential benefits. The consequent development of private property rights in land was a gradual process stretching over centuries.

Protection of production and transportation of goods and services was another requirement of an exchange economy. Originally, individual artisans and merchants protected their own goods; but, as noted in Chapter II, this protection could be undertaken more cheaply by a government than by each individual. We should not forget, however, that while artisans and merchants as a group stood to gain by the state's taking over protection of property rights, each individual had an incentive to let others pay for this *public good.*

In the meantime "the state" was changing, too. The local manorial lord typically provided protection and "law" in feudal society. But an exchange economy not only made local protection inefficient and useless for trade beyond the confines of the manor, but also led to another consequence that would transform Europe: it altered the scale of warfare. In feudal times a vassal provided knight's services to a superior lord for 40 days a year. Given such limitations, large permanent armies were impossible. Moreover, a distant army was no protection against marauding bands of Huns, Magyars, or Vikings. The local castle was the source of protection. However, when vassals paid money to superior lords, in lieu of knight's services, then lords could hire mercenaries, and the lord with the greatest resources could put the largest army in the field. New weapons also transformed military activity. The longbow and the pike, then gunpowder, cannon, and musket made the heavily armored knight and the castle obsolete. All this required a vast increase in fiscal revenues, and the only place to get these revenues was from the private sector. Princes vied with each other in providing protection or granting property rights in return for the revenues necessary to survive in an age of intrigue, conspiracy, shifting alliances, and expanded warfare.

There were two important consequences to our story. (1) The minimum size for survival of the state grew enormously, and the nation-state was the logical result. (2) The fiscal needs of princes were great, but since their bargaining power with their constituents varied from one nation to another and the structure of their economies differed, widely divergent patterns of property rights emerged, with important implications for economic efficiency. In England and the Low Countries, kings were forced to give up much of their power to parliaments in return for revenues. The English Parliament gradually evolved and embedded in English common laws a set of relatively efficient property rights. In Spain and France, absolutist monarchs emerged, and immediate fiscal necessity led to the granting of guild monopolies that discouraged innovation and the more efficient allocation of factors of production. In some cases, confiscation of property drove people out of productive activity altogether.

These developments are important to our story because as the frontier movement extended across the ocean, the new settlers carried with them the institutions of their home land.

Settlement in the New World

Following Prince Henry the Navigator's early explorations along the African coast in the fifteenth century, the Portuguese, Spanish, Dutch, and English (in roughly that chronological order) explored, traded with, and settled new areas of the world (and in some cases succeeded in enslaving the indigenous population). The Spanish and the Portuguese settled in South and Central America—the Portuguese on the east, in what is now Brazil, the Spanish on the west, up through Central America and as far north as Florida. The French came, settled what is today Canada, traveled down around the Great Lakes, and followed the Mississippi River to its mouth at what is now New Orleans. The British, who came last, settled the coastal strip of North America from Maine almost to the Florida border. The colonists came over for reasons as varied as their nationalities and their temperaments —for freedom of worship, for escape from political persecution, but also purely and simply for the sake of a business venture. Obviously, the settlers who came were adventurous people. The whole undertaking involved risks unthinkable to any but the most daring, and their courage is reflected in their social attitudes, their determination to better themselves, to build a new life. The dissidents among them were continually struggling to improve not just the religious and political climates, but economic climate as well. One of the main prerequisites to development—lacking today in some underdeveloped countries, but one that we richly inherited—is the combination of social attitudes that attuned America's colonists to economic growth; they responded quickly to economic incentives, thereby making the markets for labor and capital work better, and they tried to produce goods and services in demand elsewhere. The institutions that the English settler brought with him provided a hospitable background for growth. It is true that the Virginia Company and some of the other early colonial ventures started out by working land in common, but the disastrous consequences quickly led to modification and the *de facto* development of private property rights in land.

The products of the colonial economy were those that they could make most efficiently. What a given area tends to produce efficiently will be determined by the relative costs of the factors of production: land, labor, capital, and managerial talents, which must be combined in some form to produce anything. The relative cost of each of these productive factors is determined by its relative scarcity or abundance. Abundance tends to lower the price; scarcity elevates it, as potential users bid higher. For example, if not much capital is available, but many people demand capital to construct buildings, factories, equipment, and farms, then the price of capital will be high. Similarly, if a great deal of rich, productive land is available, the price of land will be low. This is the pattern that determined the form of production in the New World. Having abundant rich land, scarce labor, and scarce capital, the colonies not surprisingly turned to agriculture, which provided the major source of economic activity for perhaps 90 percent of the population. Now set the concept of production according to comparative advantage alongside the particular natural endowments of the New World, and it becomes evident why each region developed its own characteristic economic pattern. Each region's production possibilities were different. The great incentive was to raise living standards by producing goods so efficiently that they would find a market outside the colonies and thereby make possible the import of other goods that they wanted. This desire for efficient specialization divided the colonies into three major economic areas: the South, the Middle Colonies, and New England.

Regional specialization

The South produced goods—rice and indigo in the lower part, tobacco in the upper part—that fitted ideally the sort of pattern that England had in mind for colonial settlement; that is, it produced commodities that the English did not produce and that England and other countries wanted to obtain by trade. One disadvantage appeared in this pattern, however: these agricultural goods all required not only an abundance of land, but an abundance of labor—and this was a relatively scarce and expensive factor. Indeed, it appears that in the colonial area, wages may have been as high as, or even higher than, they were in England. This led to the desire to import workers for all the colonies, most urgently for the southern plantations. Early plantation labor was supplied by free men or indentured servants, who were gradually replaced by slaves in the seventeenth century. Southern colonists accepted slavery as a means of supplying a cheap labor force to work on the plantations and to produce staple commodities in international demand. The pattern of trade and commerce of the southern colonies increasingly emphasized the export of such items, particularly to England and Europe, to finance the import of other goods. In general, the value of their exports to England exceeded the value of their imports from England and thus fitted ideally the pattern that Britain hoped to develop in colonial trade.

Turning to the Middle Colonies, we see a very different picture. These occupied the relatively fertile agricultural areas of New York, Pennsylvania, and New Jersey, where grain and livestock could be efficiently produced and where important seaports opened up access to the interior. This was a valuable combination, for at the time the only efficient way to carry goods over long distances was by water. Rich land that lay far from navigable water was handicapped by the high costs of land transport, and farmers on such land could not offer their products for sale at a profit outside their particular area. So New York and Philadelphia grew up as collection centers for the agricultural goods of the interior, as ports for shipping these goods to the rest of the world and importing other goods and services that the colonists demanded. Since the products of the Middle Colonies were by and large the things that the Englishman himself produced, the pattern of trade of these colonies came to be more with southern Europe and the West Indies than directly with England. As a matter of fact, more was imported than exported in the Middle Colonies' trade with England.

The third area, New England, was totally different again. Although most people still earned their living from the soil, the land was relatively poor (except in a few rich river valleys like the Connecticut), and a large number turned to gaining a living from the sea, which provided rich resources for fishing and whaling. As New Englanders became expert in these skills, their region matured to a major shipping power in the world, supplying ships not only for their own needs but for England as well. The colonies shipped their own goods, such as fish, to the West Indies; in addition, they carried goods of other colonies and other countries to the entire British Empire and beyond, so that shipping income became a most important factor in New England's economic well-being.

Colonial prosperity and British policy

Overall, it is clear that the colonies were genuinely thriving. Probably, on a per capita basis, they were as prosperous as the English people themselves—possibly more so. The sources of their prosperity, by and large, were a thriving, specialized agriculture, an associated, vigorous export trade that grew in per capita value, and an increasing shipping income from carrying other people's goods as well as their own.

In terms of the theory developed in Chapters I and II, it is easy to see why productivity increased in the colonies. There appears to have been little technological change, so that source of growth was probably not very important. On the other hand, abundant land forestalled the pressure of diminishing returns. The major source of growth came from economies of scale. With a small population scattered over a vast area, a great many economic activities were conducted at high levels of average cost. This was particularly true of market exchange activities—the costs of protecting and enforcing private property rights being high. Shipping, a major source of colonial income, offers a dramatic illustration. In early colonial times, ships had to be heavily armed as protection against pirates, and three months were often required to gather a cargo from scattered plantations and small ports. With the growth of trade it became worthwhile to eliminate pirates; it was equally worthwhile to develop central collection storehouses for goods to be shipped. Both the manning of ships and the turnaround time in port were reduced dramatically; in consequence, shipping productivity increased substantially in colonial times.

One problem appeared: the colonists, intent on raising their living standard, wanted to buy more goods from England and the Continent than they could finance by their exports alone, and this resulted in a drain of specie from the colonies. Paid in gold and silver for goods sold overseas, the luxury-hungry colonists tended to ship out the specie as soon as it was received, in return for imports. Since these metals were the base of the money supply, colonists sometimes complained about being short of money. What they meant was they they preferred to import more goods rather than to keep a larger money supply at home.

A deliberate British policy of control over the colonial economy began in the 1650s with the imposition of navigation laws designed to protect British shipping from that of the Dutch. Dutch shipping was the most efficient then available, increasingly carrying the world's goods, and shipping was too important a source of world income for the British to let it go lightly. Part of their answer to the Dutch challenge was the promulgation of laws requiring that ships in the British Empire trade be built and largely manned by Britons or by British colonials. They required further that certain strategic, or "enumerated," goods be shipped only to England, and trade with England grew until the Revolution (Fig. IV·1, p. 52). Tobacco was one of these goods, and Fig. IV·2 on p. 53 indicates that English merchants benefited increasingly by the receipt of all American tobacco and the reexport of a substantial part of it. It is perhaps not surprising that the colonists complained about enumeration, which will be discussed more fully later on. Next, the laws demanded that European goods en route to the colonies pass through England and the English customs—another grievance for the import-loving colonists. Fourth, the colonies were prohibited from exporting certain manufactured goods: hats, wrought iron, and some other products. Fifth, to assure Britain's independent supply of certain important commodities, a bounty was declared on such colonial products as indigo dye and the naval stores (pitch, turpentine, tar, masts) used in all kinds of naval and merchant marine activities. After 1763, when the British had just concluded a costly war and their exchequer was depleted, they felt that the colonists should shoulder an additional tax burden. The result was a number of revenue acts with names that are schoolboy history—the Stamp Act, the Townshend Act, the Sugar Act—all designed to increase taxes on the colonists. Also, measures were passed that were designed primarily to keep the colonists from crossing the Appalachian Mountains and settling in an area that the British hoped to keep out-of-bounds, to

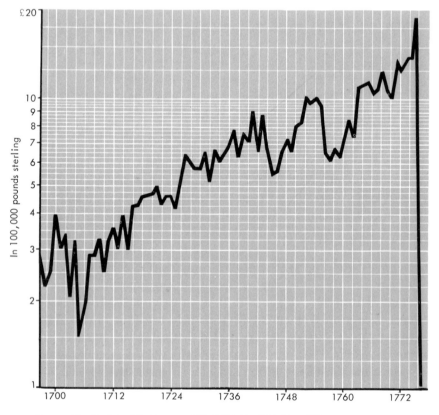

Fig. IV · 1   VALUE OF AMERICAN COLONIES' EXPORTS TO ENGLAND, 1697–1776

Source: *Hist. Statistics* (Washington : GPO, 1960), Ser. Z 21–34, p. 757.

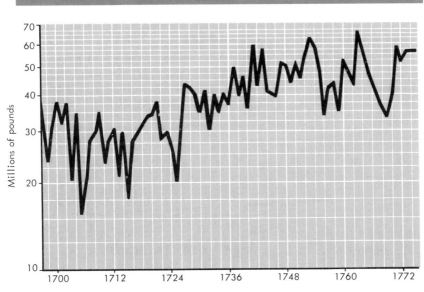

Fig. IV · 2   TOBACCO EXPORTED TO ENGLAND BY AMERICAN COLONIES, 1697–1775

Source: *Hist. Statistics* (Washington: GPO, 1960), Ser. Z 223–29, p. 765.

prevent warfare with Indian tribes. This also stirred colonial antagonism, although no one of these acts was vitally important in its economic impact on the colonists.

CAUSES OF THE REVOLUTION

Earlier in the chapter we saw how national states emerged from feudal society and undertook the protection and enforcement of property rights at a lower cost than could individuals and voluntary groups. The amount of taxes the state could collect depended upon its bargaining strength vis-à-vis its constituents. If the gains to the constituents were small and there were active competitors for providing these services (the protection and enforcement of property rights), then the state could collect little in taxes, or it would face revolt or a switch of allegiance to another potential supplier. On the other hand, if the gains were large—perhaps because all property rights were endangered by the threat of either outside invasion or internal disorder or because the state had no close competitors—then it could exact much higher taxes.

What were the costs and benefits to the colonists of being subject to British rule? There is no point in being much concerned with the problem before 1763; before that date it is doubtful that the colonists could have stood alone or would have wanted to be free. The French menaced them from the north, the Spanish from the south. But after 1763, we can look at a world in which the colonists might have been either outside or inside the British system. The actual condition was a world in which they were inside. The hypothetical alternative would be one in which they were an independent nation outside the British system.[1] How would they have fared? Not all the information needed to answer that question is available, so what we find is a partial answer based on what actually occurred in a later period—from 1783, when the colonies did indeed become independent, until 1793, when all of Europe went to war. This is a period roughly comparable to the one under consideration. Although neither an economist nor a historian ever has all the facts he would like in assessing any period or event, we do have an abundance of clues for this comparison of two periods. Let us systematically consider the important costs and benefits.

First of all, tobacco was a major source of additional income derived by the British from their relationship with the colonies. Indeed, there is no doubt that the passage of tobacco through England resulted in a substantial income for British merchants. Conversely, therefore, there is no doubt that tobacco would have returned higher incomes to the colonial grower had the colonies been independent, able to export directly to Continental markets; and this is precisely what we see in the period after 1783 during the Confederation period.

But take the next item, shipping. A free and independent nation found out after 1783 that its ability to engage in this lucrative activity was curtailed by the Navigation Acts, not only of Britain, but of all the rest of the countries of Europe. Goods could sometimes be shipped between two countries only if they were produced in one of them. A country like the new American nation, which had become one of the most efficient shipping nations in the world, lost a great comparative

---

[1] This is the hypothetical alternative which is usually implicit in a historian's analysis of the issues. In terms of the immediate sources of colonial grievances, however, it was the difference between British policy and enforcement before 1763 and after 1763 that triggered colonial discontent; the colonists, at least in the beginning, had in mind as the alternative a return to the conditions that existed prior to 1763.

advantage because of these restrictions. It is therefore probable that America's shipping income would have been lower in the hypothetical case of earlier independence, since the nation would have been excluded from the West Indies trade and also limited in trade with many other parts of the world. Shipbuilding would also have been curtailed, since, inside the Empire, Britain was a major customer. Other sources of income, our exports of rice and indigo from the lower South, decreased as a result of independence in the Confederation period.

What about the restrictions placed on colonial manufacturing? They were actually not important. It will be remembered from the earlier discussion of factor proportions that manufacturing requires comparatively large amounts of capital and labor, but little land; this was exactly the wrong combination of factors for the colonial economy, which therefore could not compete in manufacturing activities except where nearness to raw materials conferred a special advantage, as in iron production and shipbuilding. Presumably, little if any income was lost as a result of the British domination in manufacturing.

The final item to consider is the requirement that colonial imports pass through England. Here the colonists would have enjoyed somewhat better terms if they had been independent, able to trade directly with the Continent (and indeed this shows up in the Confederation period as a lowering of import prices from those of the earlier period).

The primary benefit the colonists enjoyed was the protection and enforcement of property rights provided by the British. The independent government spent annually $2,132,898 on the average for national defense in the first nine years after ratification of the Constitution. To this we must add the additional costs of conducting an independent foreign policy.

The impact of the Navigation Acts on the American colonies has been the subject of a famous (and in retrospect rather fruitless) controversy. Over thirty years ago Lawrence Harper wrote a pioneering essay entitled "The Effects of the Navigation Acts on the Thirteen Colonies."[2] He concluded that the net burden was fairly substantial. With the advent of the new economic history, Robert Thomas reexamined the issue and came to the conclusion that the net burden was "not large."[3] An apparently endless controversy ensued, the net

---

[2] Richard Morris, ed., *The Era of the American Revolution* (New York: Columbia Univ., 1939).

[3] "A Quantitative Approach to the Study of the Effects of British Imperial Policy Upon Colonial Welfare: Some Preliminary Findings," *JEH*, XXV, No. 4 (Dec. 1965).

result being that while various authors took exception to some of Thomas's methods, they all agreed with his conclusion.[4]

Where does that leave us?

1. The overall burden was "not large," but still a significant burden might have shifted to new groups who happened to be politically articulate and influential; indeed, that was probably the situation, the New England merchant being a case in point. The various acts (and retaliatory measures such as closing the port of Boston) imposed additional costs on the merchant.

2. There was no reason to believe that the burden of taxation of an independent state would fall on the same groups as in the colonies —and in fact it probably didn't. This statement is more conjecture than fact, since the necessary research has not yet been done; but a superficial examination suggests that the burden of protection was distributed quite differently after independence.

3. Clearly the overall gains to the colonists had declined since 1763. With the gradual reduction of Indian raids and the elimination of the threat of the French from the north, the benefits to the colonist were less than they had been earlier, even though they may still have been positive on balance. The direction of the change was important; but perhaps even more significant, as the literature of colonial protest makes clear, the door was now open to further increases in taxes, and that possibility was an important element in the controversy.

In terms of the framework of analysis we advanced above, the colonists saw that the benefits of British protection had fallen—that the net burdens had risen; and more important, the door had been opened to raise the burdens still further without their having a voice in the matter. In comparing the new distribution of burdens with the prospective distribution under independence, there was abundant ground for discontent and revolution. The colonists had before them the historical experience of the mother country, where the crown's control over taxes had gradually been wrested from it by Parliament, so that arbitrary changes in tax rates could not be made without consent of that (more or less) representative body.

Nothing in what I have said implies that the Revolution was necessarily a purely economic phenomenon. All *I wish* to state at this point is that the endless controversy over the net burden of the Navigation Acts has in no way settled the issue of the causes of the American Revolution. We still have some research to do to answer that question.

---

[4] See the Bibliography for a list of the combatants.

YEARS OF DECISION, 1783–1793

The years from 1783 to 1793 were a time of decision for the new American society. Politically, this was the period for choosing the form of a new government and for establishing a Constitution—both having lasted ever since. For the economy, it was a time to develop the basic rules of the game, which have continued to this day.

The new nation and *The Wealth of Nations*

The year 1776 produced not one but two documents of importance to the new nation and of fundamental significance to our history. One was, of course, the Declaration of Independence, pointing the way to national independence; the other was Adam Smith's *The Wealth of Nations*. With an insightful combination of historical observation, analysis, and polemic, Smith described the workings of a market economy and argued for an unshackled system of enterprise as the most fruitful device for enlarging "the wealth of nations."

When the war with England ended, America faced all the problems that confront any new nation. To survive, it was necessary to create a viable economy. A government must be established not only to institute the political process but to make countless decisions, not the least of them economic in nature. What should be the government's role in the economy? What responsibility should it have? How should a legal structure be developed to delineate the rights and the restrictions of private property? Where were tax revenues to come from, and how much should be collected? Also to be decided were the touchy issues of where the money should be spent. To speak of taxes is to pose a double question: who is to pay them and who is to benefit from them? When tax receipts are paid out, some people will usually gain more than others. Finally, a monetary system was needed not only to serve the fiscal purposes of the government but also to provide a medium of exchange and to develop the capital markets required in an efficient market economy.

Historically, these questions had been answered by setting up the system—really only a collection of practices—known as mercantilism, in which the government was involved in the economy in a whole variety of ways. Among other mercantilistic devices, bounties were paid to encourage the production of specified commodities, and monopolistic privileges were awarded to some companies, giving exclusive trading rights in particular areas. The aim was for the government and the economy jointly to promote national expansion and welfare— and this, as noted earlier, at the expense of other countries.

Now came Adam Smith's diametrically opposite view attacking mercantilism, arguing that it was an inefficient system, one that fostered monopoly, encouraged inefficiency, and gave special privileges to particular groups in the society. He found it to be the very antithesis of how a society should be organized to provide maximum wealth for the people of that nation. Smith argued that the main basis for economic growth was specialization and division of labor. Efficiency stemmed from employing enough people to produce a commodity, so that their tasks could be specialized and therefore more rapidly and efficiently done, since each man could concentrate on doing just one thing repetitively. Also, if his specialized task were reduced to its narrowest possible form, then machines might be developed to do his work. In short, technological change would be encouraged by specialization; and since division of labor depends on the feasibility of producing on a large enough scale, we come to the size of the market as a basic influence upon specialization. A small producer, turning out just a few items a day, a week, or a year, will probably do all the work himself; but if his market increases, he will need to have a larger number of workers. Each task can be specialized, and he can then institute a division of labor.

In a market economy, the one who organizes the economic activity is the entrepreneur or businessman. He decides what will be produced, basing his decision on the relative returns from different kinds of pursuits. If it appears that making shoes will return more than making bricks or hats or any other alternative, he will produce shoes; but to start making shoes, he needs a location, equipment, and labor. Accordingly, he may borrow the necessary capital to buy machines, to build a factory, and to advance payment to his workers while they are producing the goods. While the entrepreneur makes the decisions about what will be produced, being guided by relative profitability, the capital market plays a crucial role in financing his start in production.

Adam Smith was a bitter critic of mercantilism because he saw in it an artificial inducement for a society to produce the wrong things. Because bounties or subsidies were paid for a certain commodity, it might appear to an entrepreneur as a remunerative venture, when in society's judgment it was not. The relative returns from different kinds of activities are not only an advantageous guide to the businessman, but they are also consistent with allocating resources in order to expand the welfare of the society as a whole—that is, the most remunerative pursuits are those that produce in response to what consumers want, and therefore they are most beneficial to the society.[1] It was this reasoning that led Adam Smith to the conclusion that private self-interest—guiding the businessman into the most remunerative pursuits, the worker to the job with the highest wages, and so forth—will simultaneously promote maximum public welfare.

The issues of the 1780s

The conflict between Adam Smith's view and the mercantilist view was very much in the minds of Americans in the 1780s as they struggled to resolve the many problems they faced. Some of these problems were of staggering size. The new nation emerged from the Revolutionary War deeply in debt—to foreigners such as the French who had helped with finances, munitions, and equipment; to American citizens who had loaned the Continental Congress great sums. These debts were of such magnitude that the question was how could we pay them all. And, indeed, should they all be paid? The latter was considered a reasonable question because, in many cases, the original creditors had sold their Continental bonds at a fraction of their face value; and it was argued that since speculators had bought up these bonds at a substantial discount, they should not receive payment at face value.

---

[1] As noted in Chapter II, Adam Smith was aware of important exceptions to the equation of private with social rates of return.

The whole knotty problem of the public debt was the subject of priority debate in America's early government.

A second problem facing the economy was that the soldiers of the Revolutionary War had been promised substantial benefits. In previous wars, it had been a policy to award officers half pay for life or to pay them full pay for five years after the war. Again, who would pay for this? How could such sums be raised?

Still a third urgent demand for tax monies after the war arose because our shipping and trade now became the prey of pirates—particularly the Barbary pirates when we tried to enter the Mediterranean. Before the war, the colonies had been sheltered under the British agreement that, in effect, paid tribute to these buccaneers to safeguard British and colonial ships. Now free and a good prey for the pirates, we faced two alternatives: to pay similar tribute or to build a navy and attempt to defeat them. Either choice involved substantial costs.

An even more basic issue remained to be resolved. Should the American economy be steered toward mercantilism? Should bounties and subsidies be paid to encourage certain industries? Should manufacturing be expanded, even though it might be unprofitable, to avoid dependence on foreign countries, or should a free market decide? The conflict between Adam Smith's views and the mercantilist philosophy had reached these shores.

While considering these issues, contemporaries argued vigorously about the state of the economy. Some pictured the economy in dismal and serious depression; others maintained that its present and future prospects were not nearly so bad—indeed, that they looked rather bright. Hamilton argued strongly that conditions were poor. In *The Federalist*, Paper 15, he described the plight of the economy before the adoption of the new Constitution.

We may indeed with propriety be said to have reached almost the last stage of national humiliation. There is scarcely anything that can wound the pride or degrade the character of an independent nation which we do not experience. Are there engagements to the performance of which we are held by every tie respectable among men? These are the subjects of constant and unblushing violation. Do we owe debts to foreigners and to our own citizens contracted in a time of imminent peril for the preservation of our political existence? These remain without any proper or satisfactory provision for their discharge. . . . Are we in a condition to resent or to repel the aggression? We have neither troops, nor treasury, nor government. Are we even in a condition to remonstrate with dignity?...Are we entitled by nature and compact to a free participation in the navigation of the Mississippi? Spain excludes us from it. Is public credit an indispensable resource in time of public danger? We seem to have abandoned its cause as desperate and irretrievable. Is commerce of importance to national wealth? Ours is at the lowest point of declension. Is respectability in the eyes of foreign powers a safeguard against foreign encroachments? The imbecility of our government even forbids them to treat with us. Our ambassadors abroad are the mere pageants of mimic sovereignty....To shorten an enumeration of particulars which can afford neither pleasure nor instruction, it may in general be demanded, what indication is there of national disorder, poverty, and insignificance that could befall a community so peculiarly blessed with natural advantages as we are, which does not form a part of the dark catalogue of our public misfortunes.[2]

On the other hand, Benjamin Franklin, returning to America in 1785 after a long absence, felt that the position of the economy was not nearly as dismal as it had been described to him.

All of these were vital issues of the 1780s, and the attempt to resolve them, part and parcel of the process of thinking out the needs of the new government, anticipated the Constitutional Convention of 1787. One event in particular sparked a more rapid resolution of these problems than might otherwise have taken place. In 1786, a former captain in the Revolutionary War, Daniel Shays, led a group of discontented Massachusetts farmers in revolt against the state government, which insisted that both taxes and private debts be paid in specie, as required by law and contract. Shays' Rebellion failed, put down by the Massachusetts militia, but it shocked the new American society into realization of how fragile was the structure of law and order and how necessary it was that such problems be resolved—the same problems of taxation and contractural security previously blamed on the British. Shays' Rebellion also pointed up the need for a unified policy among all the states. In the period of the Confederation, each state had made independent decisions, particularly with respect to port entry fees for foreign ships, tonnage duties, and a variety of other commercial regulations. This had, of course, led to trade wars and regulatory retaliation among the states.

[2] Alexander Hamilton, John Jay, James Madison, *The Federalist: A Commentary on the Constitution of the United States* (New York: Modern Library, 1937), pp. 87–88.

The Constitution and Federalist policies

The idea of a stronger central government gradually emerged as the answer to these needs, and this led to calling a convention, initially aimed at overhauling the Articles of Confederation but which actually created a whole new framework of national government and legal order.

Later in this chapter we shall examine some of the broader issues of growth and welfare as they relate to the Constitution. Here we shall confine ourself to describing some of immediate implications of both the Constitution and subsequent Federalist policies for the new society. What we really want to examine with respect to the Constitution is the sum of its results, viewing it by somewhat the same standards that Adam Smith used in examining how an economy ought to work. Smith believed that the individual decisions of businessmen and workers were never motivated by anything but their own selfish desires for better standards of living. He even believed such men would have promoted monopoly if they could. But what he did conclude, with only minor qualification, was that the net result of the interaction of all these individual self-interests turned out to be a society that produced the greatest improvements in welfare and the greatest growth that was possible.

In the economic field, the Constitution took notable steps.

1. *The power to levy taxes* was delegated to the central government, making possible the undertaking of necessary continuing functions of federal authority. Among other things, the government could, for the first time, pay off the debts of the states. This was a significant step in establishing a capital market, since it gave investors confidence that loans to the government would be repaid. Private borrowers would then be forced by competition to be equally faithful in keeping their own promises to pay.

2. *The right to coin money and to regulate its value* was assigned to the federal government. Throughout our history this power has had profound effects on the performance of the economy. In the twentieth century, it has been used in systematic attempts to reduce the severity of business fluctuations.

3. *Authority over foreign affairs* was given to the federal government, so that tariffs and negotiations of treaties and agreements were no longer at the discretion of the individual states.

4. *Regulation of interstate commerce* was another area delegated to the federal government, a control that historically, to this day, has had an

enormous impact. By prohibiting the states from erecting barriers to the interstate movement of goods, this clause not only encouraged the growth of a national market, but gave the federal government constitutional authority to exercise control and regulation over economic activity.

It should be emphasized, however, that the most important contribution of the Constitution was in establishing the framework for the efficient conduct of private economic activities. It defined the protection of private property and the enforcement of contracts; it created a system of stability, of law and order, which reduced uncertainty— and returning to Adam Smith's views, it is obvious how important stability is for the functioning of a market economy. What makes the businessman willing to invest is the expectation of net returns, properly discounted for risks. If risks are great, then expected returns must be still higher in order to induce the businessman to invest; and the higher the risk, the fewer willing investors. Accordingly, the Constitution's contributions toward establishing a climate of legal and political stability, reducing uncertainty, recognizing the rights of private property, and guaranteeing the enforcement of contracts were most vital and conducive to making a market economy work well.

In 1789 when the new government came into existence, it immediately set about to rectify some of the pressing problems remaining from the Confederation period. It established uniform tonnage duties of 50 cents a ton on foreign vessels and 6 cents a ton on U.S. vessels. The differential was a way of encouraging our shipping and giving us a bargaining weapon in negotiating with foreign countries to reduce or to repeal their widespread discriminatory trade restrictions against this country. It imposed a tariff that became the main source of revenue for maintaining the new government. The tariff was only incidentally protective, although there were some who desired such protection. At this time, too, Alexander Hamilton, who was the architect of much of the early economic policy in the new nation, wrote a famous series of reports that influenced our subsequent economic policies. His "Report on Manufactures" became a classic; in it, he recommended the encouragement of manufacturing under a system of bounties and subsidies. Although this report had no immediate effect (and indeed harked back to mercantilist views), it did contain valuable insights into our economy, and it pointed the way toward American industrial development. Hamilton's "Report on Public Credit" laid the groundwork for the federal assumption of states' debts and for issuing bonds that would then pay off the creditors; these bonds, in turn, became desirable reserve assets, providing respected collateral for use in private borrowing and lending transactions. They were therefore important in helping to establish a better capital market, something we have already observed as essential in improving economic organization. Hamilton was also instrumental in paving the way toward creation of the First United States Bank, which became the means of tying the banks of the country into an overall monetary system. Opening with an initial subscription of $10 million, of which the government contributed $2 million, this became, in a sense, a bankers' bank. It acted as an agent of the government, assisted in spreading and strengthening the entire banking system, and thus contributed further toward improving the capital market.

It would be a mistake to think of Alexander Hamilton as a disciple of Adam Smith. He was too much a mercantilist to fit that mold, and the policies he recommended (particularly in the "Report on Manufactures") involved a degree of government intervention that was the very subject of criticism in *The Wealth of Nations*. But the policies of Hamilton that were adopted were those that provided the essential economic structure to make a market economy work more effectively. Their result was to reduce uncertainty and to help create the fundamental conditions for an efficient capital market.

THE CONSTITUTION AND GROWTH AND WELFARE

Of the many volumes written about the Constitutional Convention, one that has profoundly shaped our evaluation is Charles Beard's *The Economic Interpretation of the Constitution*. Looking at the background of the people who dominated the convention, Beard contended that they wrote a Constitution aimed at protecting their own interests. Moreover, since class interests were the predominant basis of their individual actions, it was essentially a class document. Although this view has been widely accepted by political scientists, it has also been challenged in recent years.

Employing the framework of analysis briefly developed in Chapter II, let us see what we can say about the implications of the Constitution for growth and welfare. For promoting economic growth, the most efficient government would be one that attempted to equate private and social benefits and costs. However, since we have seen that these differ essentially because of transaction costs, an "efficient" government would act only where it had an advantage over private voluntary organizations in conducting transactions. Relevant examples were presented in Chapter II. Protection of property rights, administration of justice, and provision of defense are activities in which economies of scale and the "free rider" problem have led to collective action. But we can go further. Given any level of technology (which determines the costs of establishing and enforcing property rights), an efficient Constitution will devise a set of rules to equate the private and social rates of return and to assign to collective (government) action only those activities that can be more efficiently performed by government. It's hard to imagine that our founding fathers could have done better on this score. The Constitution, subsequent Federalist enactments, and the decisions of the Marshall-dominated Supreme Court provided a hospitable framework for economic growth in the nineteenth century.[3] But even as we find clear evidence of the Constitution's adequacy in the nineteenth century, we are led to question two crucial issues: (1) What were the implications of the Constitution for the distribution of income? (2) How responsive was the Constitution to changes in technology and economic structure that would alter the efficient mix between the private sector and the government?

An answer to the first question is surely one that should preoccupy economic historians. Was the Constitution, as Beard contended, an instrument of class domination? Was the distribution of income made more unequal in the nineteenth century, under the Constitution, than it would have been under British colonial existence? Certainly Madison was preoccupied with these issues in *The Federalist,* Paper 10. To make income redistribution extremely costly was an important reason behind devising a Constitution that formed a "Compound Republic"[4] in which legislative, judicial, and executive powers were separated, as were the powers of federal and state governments. Madison was concerned about "factions," and it is worth quoting him at some length in order to get the flavor and intent of his argument.

The most common and durable source of factions has been the various and unequal distribution of property. Those who hold and those who are without

---

[3] For a description, see Douglass North and Lance Davis, *Institutional Change and American Economic Growth* (Cambridge: Cambridge Univ., 1971), Chapters IV and XI, and Robert Higgs, *The Transformation of the American Economy, 1865–1914* (New York: Wiley, 1971), pp. 50–57.

[4] The term comes from Vincent Ostrom, *The Compound Republic* (Public Choice, 1971).

property have ever formed distinct interests in society. Those who are creditors, and those who are debtors, fall under a like discrimination. A landed
interest, a manufacturing interest, a mercantile interest, a moneyed interest,
with many lesser interests, grow up of necessity in civilized nations, and
divide them into different classes, actuated by different sentiments and
views. The regulation of these various and interfering interests forms the
principal task of modern legislation, and involves the spirit of party and
faction in the necessary and ordinary operations of the government. . . .

The inference to which we are brought is, that the causes of faction cannot
be removed, and that relief is only to be sought in the means of controlling
its effects.

If a faction consists of less than a majority, relief is supplied by the repub-
lican principle, which enables the majority to defeat its sinister views by
regular vote. It may clog the administration, it may convulse the society;
but it will be unable to execute and mask its violence under the forms of
the Constitution. When a majority is included in a faction, the form of
popular government, on the other hand, enables it to sacrifice to its ruling
passion or interest both the public good and the rights of other citizens. To
secure the public good and private rights against the danger of such a faction, and at the same time to preserve the spirit and the form of popular
government, is then the great object to which our inquiries are directed.

Madison viewed the distribution of wealth as the most durable
source of conflict but certainly not the only one, and the simplistic
notion of a class state is consistent neither with Madison's intent nor
with the history of conflicting factions since Madison's times. Obviously
Madison was concerned about the redistribution of wealth. Since the
establishment of voting requirements was left to the states, which
usually imposed property qualifications, the effect was to withhold
the franchise from the poorest members of the society. Clearly the new
Constitution made it more costly to redistribute wealth from the rich
to the poor than vice versa. But it is equally obvious that this was not
the prime consideration of the makers of the Constitution. The prime
consideration, if we take Madison at his word, was to make all redistributive efforts by factions (of whatever kind) costly and to provide
a framework that would encourage productive pursuits (i.e., that
would make private and social costs and benefits more equal) instead
of redistributive efforts. In subsequent chapters we shall see how these
relative costs have changed with the extension of the franchise and
the changing structure of the economy.

This leads us to the second question. The intent of the framers of
the Constitution was to make it extremely costly to alter the Constitution. Justice Marshall's court provided the early interpretative limits

that persisted throughout most of the nineteenth century. But it is doubtful that Marshall envisioned the complex industrial society that would emerge by the end of the nineteenth century. Stated succinctly, the private property rights that permitted efficient transactions in an essentially rural, agrarian society were quite different from those required in a complex, interdependent, urban-industrial society. However, it is equally unlikely that Marshall foresaw that the Constitution would be altered primarily by the Justices themselves, through their changing interpretations, rather than by the ponderous machinery of Constitutional amendment. We shall return to this issue, too, in subsequent chapters. We can certainly agree that devising efficient property rights in the twentieth century is vastly more complicated than it was in the eighteenth century. But we may question whether the remarkable judicial reverses in Constitutional interpretation that have characterized our modern era are either wise or efficient.

VI

AMERICAN EXPANSION, 1790–1860

By 1790, the political crisis had been resolved, and the economy was enjoying more prosperity than it had known since pre-Revolutionary days. Certainly with an unlimited supply of rich lands and an energetic populace, its long-run prospects appeared excellent. Yet there was no immediate prospect of very rapid growth. The reason for this paradox was that the domestic economy was then so small and scattered that the home market was very limited, while the foreign market was circumscribed by the Navigation Acts and by the mercantilist policies of the countries with which the new nation dealt.

The economy in 1790

The population in 1790 was less than four million, of whom almost 700,000 were slaves. It was almost evenly divided between North and South, with somewhat more than 200,000 living across the mountains in new territories that had just been opened. Only 5 percent of the people were listed as urban. There were no cities of 50,000 and only two between 25,000 and 50,000—New York and Philadelphia. This small and scattered population did not provide a very substantial market for expansion. Of that great majority of the populace who lived outside the cities, many were not a part of the market, since they neither produced crops for sale nor bought commodities on any regular basis.

We have already observed the vicissitudes of the new nation's foreign trade. While it expanded and grew from the lean years of the early 1780s, on a per capita basis it was still well below the prosperous years that preceded the Revolution. Thomas Jefferson in his capacity as Secretary of State summarized some of the obstacles to our trade.

First. In Europe—

Our breadstuff is at most times under prohibitory duties in England, and considerably dutied on re-exportation from Spain to her colonies.

Our tobaccos are heavily dutied in England, Sweden, France and prohibited in Spain and Portugal.

Our rice is heavily dutied in England and Sweden and prohibited in Portugal.

Our fish and salted provisions are prohibited in England, and under prohibitory duties in France.

Our whale oils are prohibited in England and Portugal. And our vessels are denied naturalization in England, and of late, in France.

Second. In the West Indies—

All intercourse is prohibited with the possessions of Spain and Portugal.

Our salted provisions and fish are prohibited by England.

Our salted pork and breadstuff (except maize) are received under temporary laws only in the dominions of France, and our salted fish pays there a weighty duty.

Third. In the article of navigation—

Our own carriage of our own tobacco is heavily dutied in Sweden, and lately in France.

We can carry no article, not of our own production, to the British ports in Europe. Nor even our own produce to her American possessions.

. . . Our ships, though purchased and navigated by their own subjects, are not permitted to be used, even in their trade with us.

While the vessels of other nations are secured by standing laws, which cannot be altered but by the concurrent will of the three branches of the British legislature, in carrying thither any produce or manufacture of the country to which they belong, which may be lawfully carried in any vessels, ours, with the same prohibition of what is foreign, are further prohibited by a standing law (12 Car. 2, 18. sect. 3.) from carrying thither all and any of our own domestic productions and manufactures. A subsequent act, indeed, has authorized their executive to permit the carriage of our own productions in our own bottoms at its sole discretion; and the permission has been given from year to year by proclamation, but subject every moment to be withdrawn on that single will, in which event, our vessels, having any thing on board, stand interdicted from the entry of all British ports. The disadvantage of a tenure which may be so suddenly discontinued was experienced by our merchants on a late occasion (April 12, 1792) when an official notification that this law would be strictly enforced, gave them just apprehensions for the fate of their vessels and cargoes dispatched or destined to the ports of Great Britain. The minister of that court, indeed, frankly expressed his personal conviction, that the words of the order went farther than was intended, and so he afterwards officially informed us; but the embarrassments of the moment were real and great, and the possibility of their renewal lays our commerce to that country under the same species of discouragement as to other countries, where it is regulated by a single legislator; and the distinction is too remarkable not to be noticed, that our navigation is excluded from the security of fixed laws, while that security is given to the navigation of others.

Our vessels pay in their ports one shilling and nine pence, sterling, per ton, light and trinity dues, more than is paid by British ships, except in the port of London, where they pay the same as British.

The greater part of what they receive from us is re-exported to other countries, under the useless charges of an intermediate deposite, and double voyage.[1]

Even in shipping, where America had an obvious comparative advantage over other countries, only 59 percent of her trade was carried in American bottoms in 1790 and only 63 percent by 1792.

American expansion in a world at war

The year 1793 was a doubly significant one in American economic history. Eli Whitney invented the cotton gin and Britain went to war with France, a war that lasted (with one major interruption) until 1815. The cotton gin established cotton as the dominant interest in the South and a main source of the United States' economic activity; Britain's war with France, more immediately important to our economy, tied up the shipping and trade of England, France, and most European countries and gave the neutral United States an overwhelming advantage in carrying on much of the world's trade. At one fell swoop, all the restrictions of Navigation Acts and mercantilist policies were removed from the American carrying trade. We transported sugar, coffee, cocoa, pepper, spices, and other commodities from the tropical and subtropical parts of the world to Europe, and in turn brought manufactured goods from Europe to the rest of the world. On top of that, our own domestic exports increased, particularly as cotton spread over the South in response to the demand from the new cotton textile mills growing apace in England. The results can be seen in Figs. VI·1 and VI·2 (Figure VI·1 shows the growth of total exports and reexports: goods were brought into the United States and then reexported to Europe or brought from Europe and reexported to colonies. Figure VI·2 indicates the growth of net shipping earnings from the U.S. carrying trade.

In addition to the rapid expansion in shipping earnings, prices

---

[1] Thomas Jefferson, "Report of Secretary of State on the privileges and restrictions on the commerce of the United States in foreign countries," Report to the 3rd Cong., 1st Sess., Dec. 16, 1793, printed in *American State Papers, 1789–1794*, I (Boston, 1817), pp. 431–32; 428.

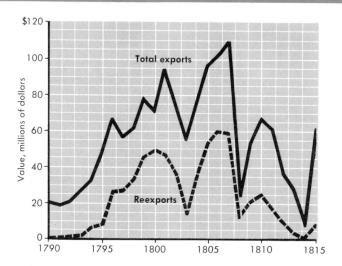

Fig. VI · 1   VALUE OF EXPORTS AND REEXPORTS FROM U.S., 1790–1815

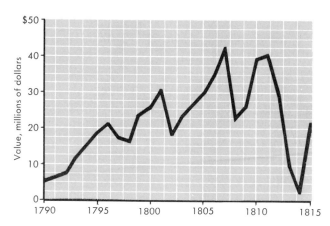

Fig. VI · 2   NET FREIGHT EARNINGS OF U.S. CARRYING TRADE, 1790–1815

Source: Both charts from Douglass C. North, *The Economic Growth of the United States, 1790–1860*, pp. 26, 28.

paid for our exports now bought more imports than before, because the price of imports had not risen as much as that of exports. The effect on our terms of trade is seen in Fig. VI·3.[2]

This expansion of trade and shipping was not accomplished without severe trial and tribulations. Both sides in the war were unhappy with America's role; and in 1797 and 1798, French seizures of our ships on the one hand and talks of peace on the other led to a fall in shipping activities. Peace came in 1801, and until 1803 there was another precipitous drop in our trading activity as European nations again carried their own trade. From 1803 to 1807 the United States experienced another period of turbulent expansion. The end was already in sight in 1805, however, with the Essex decision, in which the British reverted to a 1756 rule that neutrals in time of war could carry only the goods that they had carried during time of peace. Between this rule and Napoleon's Berlin decree attempting to blockade Britain, the end of our lucrative expansion was near. Jefferson, fearing that if we continued our shipping we would become involved in the war, declared an embargo, which was followed by the precipitous decline observed in 1808. Shipping and trade partially recovered between 1809 and 1812, although never completely nor to the level of prosperity enjoyed before 1807. Then, with America's actual entry into the conflict in 1812, the British blockade effectively eliminated most of our external trade until the end of that war.

There can be no doubt that the years 1793 through 1807 were extraordinarily prosperous for the American economy. The fact appears in the numerous literary descriptions by people who observed the economy during that time and in the few figures we do have—such as urbanization increasing from 5 to 7.3 percent and rapid expansion of the major cities (Baltimore, Boston, New York, and Philadelphia) between 1790 and 1810. There can also be little doubt that the period between 1793 and 1808 was one of full employment, in which our resources were utilized completely. A substantial increase in productivity resulted particularly from the growth in size of the market. That growth, in turn, was stimulated as the high prices being paid for our exports attracted America's agricultural products into the marketplace and made it possible for farmers to specialize in producing, thereby pulling them out of selfsufficiency and into the market economy. Moreover, the temporary phenomenon of very high export prices

---

[2] The terms of trade (net barter) are obtained by dividing a price index of imports into a price index of exports.

Fig. VI · 3   U.S. TERMS OF TRADE, 1790–1815

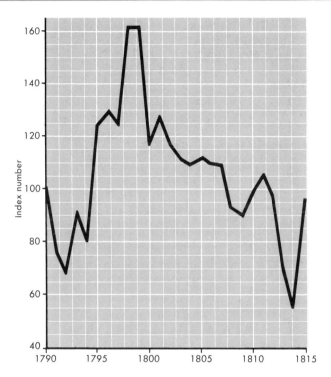

Source: Douglass C. North, *The Economic Growth of the United States, 1790–1860*, p. 31.

coupled with very low import prices (reflecting the situation of a world at war) meant that, at least for this very brief period, we became better off than ever before, as a result of being able to buy more manufactured imports with every dollar of exports.[3]

With the embargo, this prosperity came to an end, and the year 1808 was characterized by depression and unemployment that reached the seacoast and the market-oriented sectors of the American economy. Despite some relaxation of the embargo, with subsequent acts designed to stimulate trade with one or another of the belligerents, we never completely recovered in the years 1808 to 1812, and a good deal of the capital that businessmen had invested in shipping now turned instead into manufacturing. The embargo meant not merely that we did not sell to belligerents—we could not buy from them, either. As a

[3] It should be noted, however, that favorable terms of trade do not necessarily imply any improvement in the income position of a country. This was an extraordinary situation.

result, the prices of manufactured goods rose dramatically, encouraging businessmen to put their capital where the profits were. Consequently, where before 1808 only 15 cotton mills had been built in the United States, by the end of 1809 there were 87 additional mills, and this expansion continued right up through the War of 1812. Similar activity spread far afield into manufacturing a variety of other kinds of goods formerly imported.

It is clear that American capital would at that time have been more profitably employed, however, if it could have been used in shipping, and the earnings from that shipping then used to buy British manufactures. The British, with their relatively cheaper capital and skilled labor, could produce such goods more cheaply than we could. By the same token, we enjoyed advantages in shipping. The embargo, therefore, had forced us for a time into an inefficient course. American manufacturing developed prematurely, thriving only under the artificial protection of the embargo and the war. When the War of 1812 ended, England's more efficiently-produced exports became shattering competition, causing a drastic decline in American manufacturing.

Even during the years 1808 to 1814, the economy was less prosperous with this more inefficient orientation of production than it had been in the booming period prior to the embargo. In addition to our resources being employed less efficiently between 1808 and 1814, for a time there was substantial unemployment, and eventually we became involved in a war, with all that meant in terms of dislocation of economic activity in the United States.

The economy after the second war with England

When America emerged in 1815 from the second war with England, its position was somewhat analogous to that of 1790. This was still a small newcomer among the nations of the world. Although its population had increased from not quite 4,000,000 in 1790 to about 8,400,000 in 1815, the citizenry was scattered over a vast area; approximately half lived in the North and half in the South, and by now a substantial total of more than one million adventurous souls had moved across the Appalachian Mountains and settled in the new West. Many of these had come in the wake of the Lewis and Clark expedition of 1803, which gave evidence of untold prospects for new settlement and development in the lands acquired from the French in the Louisiana Purchase at the beginning of the nineteenth century.

While the vast, promising, unsettled reaches of the West now added a potential asset of unknown value to the scattered settlement up and down the coast of the United States, another aspect of the economy had changed little since 1790. This was our relationship to foreign countries. By and large, the things we did best—shipping and exporting our agricultural commodities—were circumscribed by the navigation laws and by the mercantilist policies that still dominated most of Europe. Our international trade seemed to be reverting to the kinds of restrictions faced in 1790; however, there was one significant difference—cotton. When Eli Whitney invented the cotton gin in 1793, he changed the face of the South. His innovation became the main-spring of the southern economy, encouraged the perpetuation of slav-ery, and ultimately helped to promote the conflict that was to engulf America in 1861. Cotton rapidly dominated southern agriculture wherever its planting was feasible, so that the once rather diversified southern agriculture now became concentrated in cotton production in many areas. Exceptions were coastal South Carolina, where rice remained of major importance, southern Louisiana, with its sugar cane, and the upper South, where tobacco was gradually giving way to more diversified farming.[4] But cotton made the big difference in the econo-my after 1815, ruling as king in the South and exerting an important influence in the national pattern of development.

Before we look at the pattern of interregional dependence that developed from such southern specialization, we should recall that Jefferson's embargo sent a good deal of dispossessed American capital and other resources into manufacturing. Production of cotton textiles, machinery, and equipment expanded so rapidly in America between 1808 and 1814 that many people were optimistically contemplating industrialization as an accomplished fact. We know now that a peace-time economy revealed our inadequacies. Bankruptcies spread as English textiles and other manufactured products flooded into the United States and effectively undersold the higher-cost manufactures produced locally. Clearly, America lacked British manufacturing effi-ciency and was not yet ready to claim any birthright as a manufac-turing nation. With some exceptions (as Waltham Mills, discussed later), this was a period of readjustment for American industry.

The early nineteenth century found the South exporting its cotton to England. Britain at this time was in the midst of the Industrial

---

[4] Cotton, tobacco, rice, and sugar were the major cash crops for sale outside the region; however, it is well to remember that the South continued to produce substantial amounts of corn, oats, and other agricultural products, too.

Revolution, and the prime products of the new factory system were vast quantities of cotton textiles. A growing demand for raw cotton naturally resulted; and this demand, America—more preeminently than any other country in the world—was able to meet. Whenever supply did not keep pace with demand, cotton prices soared, and planters were induced to put more of their acreage into cotton.

The spread of the cotton economy of the South and the development of the cotton export trade comprise a well-known, clear story. Less well understood is the pattern of regional interdependence among the South, the West, and the Northeast. We do know that first a large fleet of flatboats and then numerous steamboats carried the produce of the new West to New Orleans. But were the corn, wheat, and meat products destined for southern markets or were they transferred to the Northeast or exported to the West Indies and other foreign markets? The subject of West-South trade has been a major issue of recent research; further studies are now in progress. At this point the weight of the evidence suggests that the importance of trade between the West and the South has been exaggerated. Per capita production of foodstuffs in the South suggests no overall need for dependence on the West, and individual plantation records are equally convincing in their evidence of relative self-sufficiency in foodstuffs. Whether or not there was more regional specialization in years of high cotton prices (and therefore more dependence on western foodstuffs) is still an unresolved question. But it appears likely that the western trade down the Mississippi was destined largely for the Northeast and foreign markets, in addition to meeting southern needs.

From the beginning of the cotton trade, the Northeast had provided shipping and insurance and had gradually found in the South and West a growing market for manufactures. As it became increasingly a deficit food area, the Northeast received foodstuffs from the West, at first via the Mississippi and by coastal vessels to eastern ports, later—especially after the 1840s—by shipment via the Great Lakes and the Erie Canal. Since cotton textiles were a major part of eastern manufactures, cotton exports to the Northeast were also a growing part of this regionally interdependent relationship.[5]

---

[5] The importance of early tariff legislation in the revival of manufacturing has been a much debated subject. The acts of 1816, 1824, and 1828 all provided protection and with the fall in prices after 1818 were probably important in the revival of some branches of the textile industry; but by 1830 the U.S. was exporting textiles and was able to stand on its own feet. In addition, the high transport costs into the interior provided protection for the early iron industry in western Pennsylvania between 1820 and 1837.

Regional specialization and development

To discover why the pattern developed requires a look in more detail at each of the separate regions. It was the behavior of prices that decided the way southern development was to take place, and Fig. VI·4 fortifies this view. It shows the prices of cotton in relation to the sales of lands in the new Southwest (Arkansas, Louisiana, Mississippi, Alabama, and Florida). Note the coincidence between periods of high prices and periods of high sales of new lands in the Southwest. In each of these periods, higher prices for agricultural commodities (in this case, cotton) lured planters, with their slaves, into the new, fertile land of the Southwest in quest of high returns from cotton cultivation. (The same pattern applied to the West, with different kinds of com-

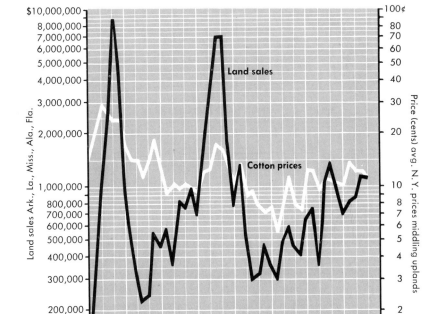

Fig. VI·4   PUBLIC LAND SALES AND COTTON PRICES, 1814–1860

Source: Douglass C. North, *T e Economic Growth of the United States, 1790–1860*, p. 124.

modities.) Therefore, the expansion in the South over this period was induced by the growing demand for cotton in Europe, leading to rising prices, to surges of expansion into the new Southwest, and to an ever-increasing supply of cotton. The British helped to finance this expansion into new cotton land by making loans to banks in Louisiana and Mississippi; the banks, in turn, financed planters in opening up these new lands.

Although some early western settlement had occurred soon after the Revolutionary War, the opening of a far-reaching transportation network stimulated a much greater westward movement. The first link was forged from the Mississippi, the Missouri, and the Ohio; along these waters and their many tributaries, the products of the West could flow to the South and thence to the Northeast or to foreign markets. Later, canals opened other parts of the West and, even more importantly, connected the whole region with the East Coast—with construction again in part financed by British capital.

The West was able to produce remuneratively both cereals and commodities derived from cereals. Wheat, corn, and livestock products were the mainstays of the western economy. As decades wore on and better transport facilities became available, a growing demand expanded the direct movement of these goods into the East itself.

The West, however, was more diversified than the South. For example, lead was found in early Missouri, and a substantial downriver trade developed as ore was carried to New Orleans and exported. Similarly, copper in Michigan and iron ore in western Pennsylvania produced early patterns of mining activity, and the iron industry itself flourished in western Pennsylvania, southern Ohio, and northern Kentucky. So while the South concentrated with single-minded attention on its cotton production, the West early reached out into more diversified economic activity.

A familiar pattern emerges in Fig. VI·5, where wheat and corn prices are compared with sales of land in seven western states. As with southern cotton, so with western wheat: rising prices induced mass movement into new lands. In the West, the expansion was into the rich lands of Ohio, Illinois, Indiana, Michigan, Iowa, Wisconsin, and Missouri. Output of western agricultural goods responded to price increases induced by the growing demand from the East and later (beginning with the Irish famine in 1844–1846) from Europe. With an expanding transportation network, the West was able to realize its potential in a pattern of interregional trade based on market-oriented

Fig. VI · 5 LAND SALES IN SEVEN WESTERN STATES, 1815–1860

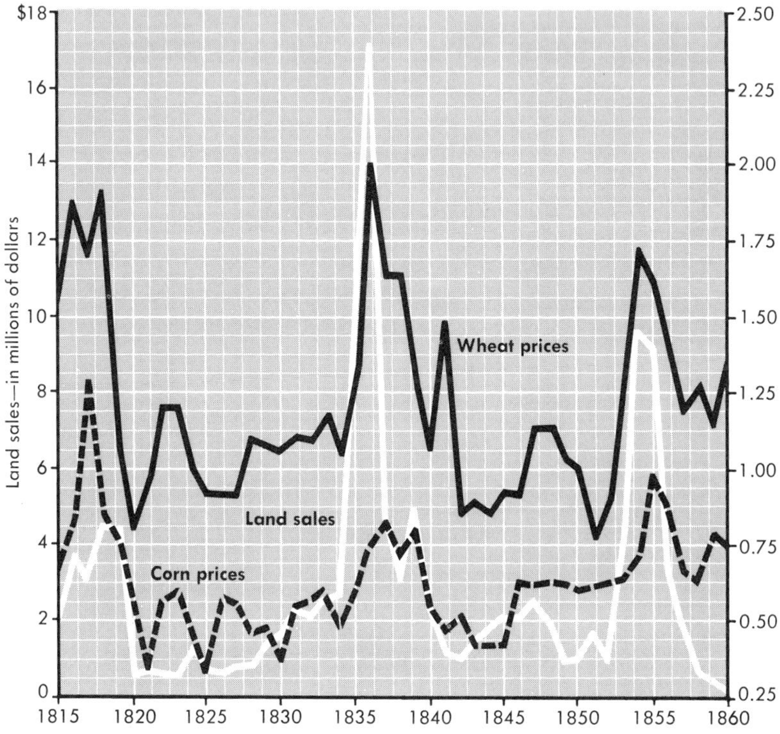

Source: Douglass C. North, *The Economic Growth of the United States, 1790–1860*, p. 137.

production. Parenthetically, the West—already more diversified than the South—was destined to become a more broadly based economy and one in which manufacturing would later develop.

In 1820, the Northeast was just recovering from its abortive industrialization, crushed by British competition. The area was still dependent upon commerce, shipping, and agriculture during this period; in fact, even though relatively declining in significance, the shipping and commerce sector continued to be an important source of income in the Northeast all through the nineteenth century. This was especially true in the period between 1815 and 1860. American ships and their goods were trading all over the world, and the merchants of Boston, Salem, and other ports along the East Coast were active in trade in every part of the globe, from China and India to Africa and all parts of Europe. Agriculture, fishing, and even whaling continued in the nineteenth century to hold a place of importance in the Northeast economy.

But the most interesting and significant development in the period between 1815 and 1860 was first the gradual, then the dramatically vigorous revival of manufacturing. It began with a slow stirring in the 1820s (although much more strongly in Massachusetts than elsewhere); then in the 1830s, manufacturing—particularly of cotton textiles—rapidly gained momentum all through southern New England, in New York, and to a lesser extent in Pennsylvania. Coincident with the growth of textiles, the iron industry, machinery production, and a variety of other manufactures also evolved during this period, reflecting the beginning of a diversified manufacturing activity. The ten leading types of manufacturing in America in 1860 are shown in Table VI·1. These are essentially of two kinds, one being oriented to resource

TABLE VI·1 LEADING BRANCHES OF MANUFACTURE IN THE UNITED STATES, 1860

Item	Employment ▼	Value of product (000s of $) ▼	Value added by manufacture (000s of $) ▼	Rank by value added ▼
1. Flour and meal	27,682	$248,580	$40,083	4
2. Cotton goods	114,955	107,338	54,671	1
3. Lumber	75,595	104,928	53,570	2
4. Boots and shoes	123,026	91,889	49,161	3
5. Men's clothing	114,800	80,831	36,681	5
6. Iron (cast, forged, rolled, wrought)	48,975	73,175	35,689	6
7. Leather	22,679	67,306	22,786	9
8. Woolen goods	40,597	60,685	25,030	8
9. Liquors	12,706	56,589	21,667	10
10. Machinery	41,223	52,010	32,566	7

Source: U.S. Census Bureau, *Eighth Census of the United States, 1860, Manufactures* (Washington: GPO, 1865), pp. 733–42.

industries—that is, dealing in the processing of resources such as the production of flour and cornmeal from wheat and corn. This substantial part of northeastern manufacturing typically developed at geographical locations where grain from the farms was brought for transshipment. Lumbering was another important resource-oriented industry.

The second group of manufactures that had evolved by 1860 comprised light manufacturing. Cotton goods stand out in the data; so do boots and shoes, men's clothing, leather, and woolen goods; and machinery is destined for still further expansion. A rather broad pattern of manufacturing had evolved in the Northeast by 1860, with cotton textiles in the vanguard. A pioneer in this industry, the Waltham Mills, was established in 1813 in Massachusetts during the second war with England. The flood of English textiles that followed the peace treaty of the following year did not bankrupt the Waltham Mills, as it did many other textile firms. Their success stemmed primarily from large-scale production, coupled with production of what was called a coarse sheeting, a cheap and simple cotton cloth that a frontier, pioneering society could put to use in all kinds of finished cotton textile goods. In addition, the English power loom was adapted to American needs and put to work in the Waltham Mills (forshadowing the continuous modification of British technology to fit American conditions). Thus, with lowgrade cotton fabric being produced by efficient technology and on a large scale, a mill was established, managed to survive even during the years 1816 to 1819, and actually did rather well. Although this was an exceptional case, the underlying conditions favorable to manufacturing expansion were gradually changing.

One element had not changed: labor and capital were still in relatively short supply in this country and were therefore relatively costly. Wages were very high, compared to those in England, and capital was also more expensive. Early manufacturing had to find some offset for the high cost of these two largest ingredients if it wished to compete. As in the case of the the Waltham Mills, one workable approach proved to be the adaptation and modification of British machinery and equipment to our particular resource endowments. Progress was made whenever a machine could be devised to economize on high-priced labor by utilizing richly abundant natural resources such as waterpower or wood. It was this ability to innovate and to modify the British improvement, coupled with the growing size of the American market, that reduced our manufacturing costs as compared to England's. The mills and factories could now begin to produce on a large enough and efficient enough scale to compete with foreign imports.

The sources of expansion

To return to the question that began this chapter—what accounts for the expansion of the economy between 1790 and 1860?—and to fit together some of the pieces of an answer, we must first observe that industrialization in the Northeast, though important, cannot claim full credit. In fact, it is clear that all three major regions contributed. In both the West and the South, incomes rose with more productive agriculture and with migration into new and richer lands. In the West, a growing market orientation led to greater specialization and division of labor. Whatever may be thought of an economy based on slavery, there is no doubt that income in the South was rising, that cotton production was growing apace, and that as a result there was also development. It was the whole American economy that was responsible for the growth, since productivity was increasing in each region.

In terms of the characteristics discussed earlier as determinants of productivity change, investment in skills and knowledge played an important role. Skilled engineers, craftsmen, and technicians—not, in those days, formally educated men, but graduates of the Yankee schools of experience—came forward to adapt and modify the techniques of Britain for American use; ingenious craftsmen, carpenters, and mechanics were the people who typically made the significant innovations. Formal education, too, was comparatively common. Table VI·2 shows the ratio of students to total population in the United States and in New England, compared with other parts of the world. Human capital accumulation provided the essential skilled labor force that was so important for high levels of productivity in both manufacturing and agriculture. The second factor, technological progress, includes some indigenous innovations like the cotton gin of Eli Whitney, which transformed a whole region, as well as the prosaic sewing machine, which played an important role in both the industrial and the household economies. Finally, increasing efficiency of organization was important and is really a central theme of this chapter. Regional specialization and the growth of interregional trade encouraged the shift out of self-sufficiency into the market economy (with resulting improvements in efficiency), created larger markets, so that economies of scale were achieved, and encouraged the improvement of factor and product markets.

**TABLE VI · 2   INTERNATIONAL COMPARISON OF RELATIVE
SCHOOL POPULATIONS, 1850**

	Ratio of students to total population ▼
New England	25.71%
Denmark	21.73
U.S. (excluding slaves)	20.40
Sweden	17.85
Saxony	16.66
Prussia	16.12
Norway	14.28
Belgium	12.04
Great Britain (on the books)	11.76
Great Britain (in attendance Mar. 31, 1851)	14.28
France	9.52
Austria	7.29
Holland	6.99
Ireland	6.89
Greece	5.55
Russia	2.00
Portugal	1.22

Source : U.S. Census Bureau, *A Compendium of the Seventh Census*, J.D.B. DeBow, Supt. of Census (Washington, 1854), p. 148.

DID THE U.S. GROWTH RATE ACCELERATE?

Economic historians tend to identify economic growth with industrialization. They have followed the traditional line of preoccupation with England's Industrial Revolution in viewing economic growth as synonymous with industrialization. Much of the economic history of the world has been written in terms of the development of "preconditions" for industrialization and then a description of the development of manufacturing. This view has been popularized by Walt Rostow in a book entitled *The Stages of Economic Growth*,[6] which attempts to put this long-accepted view into a theoretical set of stages. The most important stage for our purposes is the one called "The Take-Off" into self-sustained economic growth; and as Rostow points out, the take-off,

[6] W. W. Rostow, *The Stages of Economic Growth: A Non-Communist Manifesto*, (Cambridge : Cambridge Univ., 1960).

which he pinpoints as the years 1843–1860 in the United States, is really a return to an old-fashioned notion about industrialization.

Rostow's findings have been so conclusively criticized on both empirical and theoretical grounds that it does not seem worth our while to repeat them here.[7] Yet he has not been alone in suggesting that the growth rate must have accelerated substantially during the first half of the nineteenth century. Others—and I was among them— reached this conclusion; however, the most cogent evidence so far developed suggests no such discontinuous change. Paul David not only persuasively negates the opinion but offers positive evidence (albeit tentative, given the nature of the available evidence) that the growth of real per capita income over the whole period 1790–1860 averaged 1.3 percent per annum.[8] Where does that leave the controversy?

Let's begin with the colonial era. Recent research suggests that there was some productivity increase, at least from 1650 on, during the colonial period. A recent study by Terry Anderson suggests that per capita real income increased in late seventeenth-century New England,[9] and Shepherd and Walton provide evidence that colonial shipping and other services increased in eighteenth-century America.[10] The prosperous years of American neutrality in a world at war from 1793 to 1807 were described above; related evidence is shown in the accompanying graph of per capita credits in the balance of payments (see Fig. VI·6).

Just how big a bulge in per capita real income occurred during this brief period is a matter of conjecture, but Paul David is probably correct in his assessment that the ground lost between 1807 and 1815 was made up by the 1820s. Thereafter the factors described above are consistent with David's conclusion of an overall real growth rate for the whole period of 1.3 percent. However, we should note that this rate is still below the 1.8 percent rate of growth of real per capita income of the post-Civil War era (1865–1914).

The most likely conclusion to be drawn from this evidence is not

---

[7] See the first edition of this book, pp. 86–89. For the *coup de grace*, see Paul David, "The Growth of Real Product in the United States before 1840: New Evidence, Controlled Conjectures," *JEH*, XXVII (June 1967), 151–97. For Rostow's response, see the Appendix B to the 2nd edition of his book (Cambridge: Cambridge Univ., 1971).

[8] David, *ibid.*

[9] Terry Anderson, "The Economic Growth of Seventeenth-Century New England: A Measurement of Regional Income" (Ph. D.diss., Univ. of Washington, 1972).

[10] James Shepherd and Gary Walton, *Shipping, Maritime Trade and Economic Development of Colonial North America* (Cambridge: Cambridge Univ., 1972).

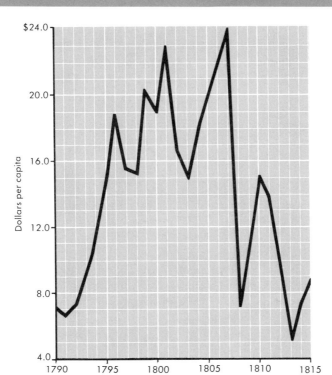

Fig. VI · 6   PER CAPITA CREDITS IN BALANCE OF PAYMENTS, 1790–1815

Source: Douglass C. North, "Early National Income Estimates of the U.S.," *EDCC*, IX, No. 3 (April 1961), 390.

that there was any discontinuous jump in the growth rate. Rather it appears likely that growth in material well-being had been occurring ever since the end of "the starving time" of colonial America and that there was gradual secular acceleration in this growth rate.

This is not really a very surprising conclusion. During colonial times, economies of scale alone should account for some increase in productivity. That is, there is a certain minimum size population necessary to produce certain goods and services efficiently, and as population increased those goods could be produced at lower and lower cost. Some of these are governmental services such as protection of property rights (against pirates on the high seas, for example) and the administration of justice. Others are privately produced (such as keeping inventories of tobacco in one place, which cut the turnaround time of ships). Indeed, it is probably correct that a growing population has resulted in substantial productivity increase via economies of scale throughout most of our history. On top of that source of growth were the factors described earlier—investment in physical and human capital, movement to better lands, shifting of labor force out of agriculture into industry, and the use of new physical capital embodying better techniques. All this was surely a gradual process cumulating over the centuries and therefore most likely to show up as a gradual increase in the growth rate.

THE ECONOMY OF
THE SOUTH, 1800–1914

The economy of the South was a subject of endless contemporary controversy in the nineteenth century, and the controversy still persists. The fact of slavery and a subsequent century in which race has continued to dominate the political, social, and economic climate have made scientific analysis difficult. As a result, much essential research remains to be done. We shall try to make a beginning in this chapter, fully aware that despite an enormous amount of writing on the subject, we still know very little. The economy of the South, particularly the postbellum economy, is now a most promising area for further research (second only to the Constitutional era) in economic history. Let's see if we can first sketch out some contours of southern economy in the nineteenth century, reserving for later consideration the parts of the puzzle that need fitting together.

The antebellum economy: description

In the years preceding the Civil War, the South concentrated heavily upon the production of a few staple commodities for sale outside the region. Cotton was by far the most important—although rice in South Carolina, sugar in Louisiana, and tobacco in the upper parts of the South were also significant export commodities. The plantation economy that characterized the production of these goods employed large amounts of land in complementary use with large amounts of labor; in the new South, accordingly, the size of the plantation was substantial, running to hundreds, and sometimes thousands, of acres.

The supply of labor was, of course, slaves. They were the major capital investment in the plantation system. Between 1802 and 1860, the price of a prime field hand rose from about $600 to about $1,800. This increase in slave prices merely reflected their increasing value in commodity production. A salient feature of the southern system was the availability of rich land to the west for extensive expansion of cotton culture; and between 1815 and 1860, planters and slaves moved westward in a series of surges that led to rapid population growth in the new Southwest. Table VII·1 shows the increase in free and slave

TABLE VII · 1	POPULATION OF FREE (BLACK AND WHITE) AND SLAVES OF ALA., ARK., FLA., LA., AND MISS ., 1820–1860				
	1820 ▼	**1830** ▼	**1840** ▼	**1850** ▼	**1860** ▼
Ala.					
F	86,622	191,978	337,224	428,779	529,121
S	41,879	117,549	253,532	342,892	435,080
Ark.					
F	12,638	25,812	77,639	162,797	324,335
S	1,617	4,576	19,935	47,100	111,115
Fla.					
F	——	19,229	28,760	48,135	78,680
S	—	15,501	25,717	39,309	61,745
La.					
F	83,857	106,251	183,959	272,953	376,276
S	69,064	109,588	168,452	244,809	331,726
Miss.					
F	42,634	70,962	180,440	296,698	354,674
S	32,814	65,659	195,211	309,878	436,631
Total (F and S)	371,125	727,105	1,470,869	2,193,300	3,039,383

Source: U.S. Congress, House *Preliminary Report on the Eighth Census*, 1860 (Washington: GPO, 1862), pp. 126–33.

population in these new states. The main surge into the Southwest occurred between 1833 and 1837, although land sales in the latter part of the 1850s did expand modestly. There were several important differences between plantations of the older areas (the Carolinas and Georgia) and those of the new Southwest. Plantations of the older areas had higher production costs of cotton and on the whole were less specialized, whereas the new plantations—particularly in Louisiana and Mississippi—tended to be highly concentrated in large-scale production of cotton or sugar.

Although we often classify the South as a plantation economy, the majority of southern whites did not own slaves. A very high proportion of them lived on small farms, and many were only peripherally related to the market. In fact, a large part of the southern population was neither regularly involved in the sale of goods nor attracted into market production during these years. With the expansion of economic opportunity in the Southwest, farmers of the Old South tended to migrate, but there was less tendency for development of local markets in the old area itself. Another striking characteristic of the South in the antebellum period was its lack of urbanization. Aside from a few ports to implement the cotton trade—such as Mobile, Savannah, Charleston, and New Orleans—there were few cities of any size. New Orleans alone gave every indication of being a thriving, growing city. In 1860 it was the only southern city among the country's top 15 in population. Along with this absence of urbanization was a lack of locally oriented industries and services, conspicuously fewer in the South than elsewhere on a per capita basis. Even retail trade, the most rudimentary of such services, was less developed than in any other area in the country. Some of these characteristics have led historians to believe that the South was a stagnating economy, but the evidence does not support this contention. Per capita income in the South (p. 90, Table VII·2) was below the national average only when slaves are included in the population. Excluding slaves, the southern income level exceeded the national average. Moreover, the trend in income during this period in the South suggests that the per capita income, far from being stagnant, was growing at a rate above the national average. A fourth characteristic of the southern economy, important for our analysis, is that investment in human capital through education was conspicuously lower in the South than elsewhere in the United States. The ratio of pupils to white population in 1840 was 5.72 percent in the slaveholding states compared to 18.41 percent in the nonslaveholding states. Illiteracy as a percentage of the white population was 7.46 percent in the slaveholding states and only 2.13 percent in the nonslaveholding states, despite the substantial numbers of illiterate immigrants who were entering the country in the North. The slaveholding states in 1850 had only slightly less than half the white population of the northern states; nevertheless, they had fewer than one-third as many public schools, one-fourth as many pupils, one-twentieth the number of public libra-

TABLE VII · 2	PERSONAL INCOME PER CAPITA IN EACH REGION AS PERCENTAGE OF U.S. AVERAGE, 1840–1950 (U.S. = 100)							
Regions ▼	**1840 ▼**	**1860 ▼**	**1880 ▼**	**1900 ▼**	**1920 ▼**	**1930 ▼**	**1940 ▼**	**1950 ▼**
NORTHEAST	135	139	141	137	132	138	124	115
New England	132	143	141	134	124	129	121	109
Mid Atlantic	136	137	141	139	134	140	124	116
NORTH CENTRAL	68	68	98	103	100	101	103	106
E. No. Central	67	69	102	106	108	111	112	112
W. No. Central	75	66	90	97	87	82	84	94
SOUTH	76	72	51	51	62	55	65	73
So. Atlantic	70	65	45	45	59	56	69	74
E. So. Central	73	68	51	49	52	48	55	62
W. So. Central	144	115	60	61	72	61	70	80
WEST			190	163	122	115	125	114
Mountain			168	139	100	83	92	96
Pacific			204	163	135	130	138	121

For footnoted details, see source: Richard A. Easterlin, "Regional Income Trends, 1840–1950," *American Economic History*, Seymour E. Harris, ed. (New York: McGraw-Hill, 1961), p. 528.

ries, one-sixth as many volumes in these libraries. Obviously, the South invested less in the education of its white people than did the rest of the United States in the years before the Civil War.

The antebellum economy: conclusion

From this very brief and summary description can be drawn some important analytical conclusions about the South. The first is an obvious one: the comparative advantage of cotton over alternative forms of production was so great that this was the rational investment for the southerner to make. In the few years around 1845, cotton's fall to 5 cents per pound was viewed as a temporary period of very low prices and not a permanent one. In general, the southerner correctly believed that his income would be higher from cotton production than it would be if he devoted his slaves, his land, and his other resources to an alternative economic activity. Second, all the characteristics of the southern picture indicate a wealth-maximizing economy in which people acted rationally. Rising returns from cotton production, a result of rising prices, led to the waves of westward movement described in

Chapter VI (see Fig. VI·4). Indeed, this points up an important factor in our whole expansion westward: the process was induced by the rising returns from commodities that were in demand in the rest of the United States and in the world beyond.

The behavior of cotton prices (Fig. VI·4) was governed by the following sequence of events. A period of relatively high cotton prices brought a surge of planters and slaves into the new Southwest. For a period of three or four years, land was cleared, and a preliminary crop of corn was sometimes planted; then, when the land was ready, cotton was planted. As its supply substantially increased, its price drastically fell, until it was no longer an inducement to westward expansion, and some of the land was switched to corn. Cotton prices tended to remain low for a rather lengthy period, however, because any increase in demand was met by a further increase in supply, since planters who had cleared the land could shift from corn back to cotton again if it became more remunerative to do so. This continued until demand increased enough to employ all the cleared land, then prices rose.

The lack of urbanization and locally oriented industry and trade in the South probably reflected two related characteristics of the southern economy. First, cotton production did not encourage additional kinds of economic activity, industry, or commerce. The planter had only to get his baled cotton to the wharf of one of the abundant waterways of the South; there the crop could be shipped out, and there, in turn, he could receive whatever imports he demanded. Indeed, the factor system—under which the New England or the English merchant bought the cotton, provided the imported goods for the planter, and carried on all necessary shipping and insurance services—relieved the planter of all commercial activities. The second characteristic that probably inhibited more diversified activities in the South concerned the distribution of income. This was obviously very unequal, with most of the labor force enslaved. The wealthy planter tended to buy imported goods and to send his children north to school, but he used few goods that would encourage local industry in the South. As for the rest of the populace, they had such low incomes and were to such a large extent self-sufficient that they could not much encourage the growth of locally oriented goods and services. Still, there is nothing about either the crop characteristics or the income level of the South that suggests an economy that was not viable or, indeed, thriving. Slavery formed the basis for an economy that achieved substantial growth and relative prosperity.

The postbellum economy[1]

The Civil War was perhaps the first modern war—modern not only in its vast military mortality but also in the widespread destruction that accompanied its ultimate conclusion. Sheridan and Sherman's celebrated marches were only episodes in the sweeping destruction of capital that accompanied the defeat of the South. The South was prostrated; but from the viewpoint of economic analysis, the two most significant events were: (1) the destruction of capital and labor already mentioned, and (2) the transformation of four million human beings from mere capital equipment into people who could choose between leisure and labor, between city and countryside—at least within limits imposed by their knowledge and their necessities. Emancipation in fact meant something less than complete freedom, but it is important to understand the magnitude of the potential transformation. The abolition of slavery did not entail any change in the total assets of the society. But a gigantic redistribution of wealth had occurred with the reality of emancipation. It had another consequence crucial to our understanding of postwar southern economy. In the prewar South, slaves were simply capital, and under these conditions the interregional flow of resources would tend to equalize the income per capita of the free population, a point we noted above when examining Table VII·2. On the other hand, the figures for the post-Civil War period mirror the fact that blacks were more or less free agents in the population. Accordingly, comparing the pre- and post-Civil War figures is misleading. Thus, the 1880 figure mirrors two important factors: (1) the very real destruction of material and human capital as a result of the war, and (2) the transformation of blacks from capital to labor. Between 1880 and 1900 we observe that per capita income grew as rapidly in the South as in the rest of the country, and in the next twenty years per capita income grew more rapidly in the South than in the country as a whole.

We must get behind the figures in order to understand the southern economy after the war. By 1880, physical output in southern agriculture had recovered in most respects to its 1860 level (exceptions were the number of swine and acres in farms); but the *value* of southern agricultural output was still below the 1860 level. On the other hand, industrial output shows a substantial increase both in number of

---

[1] For much of the analysis in this part of Chapter VII, I am indebted to my colleague, Bob Higgs. See his *The Transformation of the American Economy, 1865–1914* (New York: Wiley ,1971), Chapter V.

manufacturing establishments and in capital; indeed, even the 1870 figures exceeded those before the Civil War.[2] The growth of manufacturing in the South was substantial after 1880. By 1910 there were two-thirds as many cotton spindles in the South as there were in the North, and much of this growth was financed by northern funds. But the cotton textile industry was not the only beneficiary of northern capital. The argument suggested above would imply that given relatively scarce capital and abundant labor in the South, capital would flow into all kinds of southern activity. And that is precisely what we do observe. Textiles, iron and steel production, cotton plantations were only some of the beneficiaries. This point is important because traditional descriptions of the postbellum South have suggested a long era of stagnation in which northern capital exploited and kept the South in bondage (which implies that it delayed southern economic development). Both assertions are clearly in error.

THE SOUTHERN ECONOMY: SOME UNRESOLVED ISSUES

When the first edition of this book was being written, a major issue was the profitability and viability of slavery. The issue is still alive, and economic historians still argue about the degree to which slave breeding existed as well as about the exact numbers needed to resolve the profitability issue. Yet the issue is, if not moribund, at least on its last legs. Slavery, from most accounts and analyses, was a viable and profitable institution.[3] It's time economic historians turned to other issues, and recent research is doing just that. For example:

1) What determined the structure of the southern economy, the timing of the change in structure, and the rate of growth?
2) Was the post-Civil War sharecrop system of agriculture an "efficient" market response to the problems of southern agriculture or was it imposed to exploit southern blacks (and poor whites too, for that matter)?

---

[2] Eugene Lerner "Southern Output and Agricultural Income, 1860–1880," *The Economic Impact of the American Civil War,* ed. R. Andreano (Cambridge: Schenkman, 1967), p.110.

[3] For a summary of the issue, see R. W. Fogel and S. L. Engerman, ed., *The Reinterpretation of American Economic History* (New York: Harper 1971) Section VII. On the general issue of property rights in man, see *JEH*, March 1973.

3) To what extent does racial discrimination explain the income distribution of the South?

We shall not provide definitive answers to any of these questions, but we can at least explore the nature of the issues and indicate some recent research findings. Let's take them in order.

1) The antebellum structure of the southern economy has been at least partly explained earlier in this chapter. Two aspects of this structure appear important: one was the low level of investment in human capital; the second was the distribution of income, which militated against widespread local demand for many types of goods and inhibited urban and industrial development.[4]

Education continued to lag in the South in the post-Civil War years. There was a substantial increase in educational investment and in the percentage of children of school age who were enrolled in school, but the poor quality of the schooling and the differential between white and black schooling modified this point. The correlation between income and investment in formal education is very clear,[5] but this does not establish which way the causation runs. It does appear reasonable to expect that higher levels of education would have permitted southerners to take advantage of a wider range of opportunities.

The income distribution issue is equally conjectural. But clearly the emancipation entailed a vast redistribution of wealth and income in the postbellum South, and no matter how poor the blacks were, they were clearly better off than under slavery. By 1910, some 218,000 black farmers in the South owned all or part of their land—over 13 million acres valued at more than $300 million. This accumulation occurred in spite of the vast obstacles put in their way by discriminating whites. We have already observed that income grew as rapidly in the South as in the rest of the country between 1880 and 1910, and it appears likely that it was less unequally distributed by 1910 than it had been in 1860. If so, this, too, could have contributed to a more diversified and urbanized southern economy.

2) The southern agricultural economy in the last part of the nineteenth century has been widely regarded as a system in which the

---

[4] For a recent restatement of this argument, see W. N. Parker, "Slavery and Southern Economic Development: An Hypothesis and Some Evidence," *Agricultural History*, XLIV, No. 1, January 1970, pp. 115–27.

[5] See Lewis Solomon, "Estimates of the Costs of Schooling in 1880 and 1890," *Explorations in Economic History*, VII (Supplement), p. 534.

ex-slave was exploited and little better off than before—a new system of exploitation to replace the old. There can be no doubt that white southerners attempted to reimpose restrictions to do just that. Violence and intimidation, along with strict vagrancy laws, were designed to tie the ex-slave to the land. At the same time, however, a counterforce was in operation. Southerners were in competition for labor, and it was in the interests of an individual planter to offer a wage or a rental agreement that would attract labor. If a sufficient number of white farmers did compete, it would push up the earnings of laborers and tenants to competitive levels and eliminate "exploitation." The point is not a new one. Gary Becker pointed out some time ago that discrimination is costly to whites and blacks.[6] Robert Higgs recently published data showing that wage differentials between white and black farm workers in the South at the turn of the century were small, if indeed such differentials existed at all.[7] When we examine farm tenancy, we observe that black tenants had smaller farms than white tenants had, even after we have standardized comparisons by adjusting for several variables associated with farm size. These results may imply racial discrimination in the land rental market, but until we learn more about relative black/white productivity, it is impossible to say.[8]

3) Just how effective was discrimination? The issue is not whether or not discrimination affected income distribution. It obviously did. The issue is *how much* did it affect income distribution, what mechanisms of discrimination were effective and what were not effective, and how did they change over time? It is clear that white-dominated police and courts weakened black property rights; and perhaps most important of all, differential educational opportunities provided blacks with lower levels of skill and knowledge than whites could acquire.[9] Thus, despite the market forces that made discrimination expensive and the obvious gains that blacks made in the last part of the nineteenth century, the whole issue is still far from resolved. Any explanation of the persistence of black–white differences in income right up to the present requires a systematic exploration of these historical issues.

[6] *The Economics of Discrimination* (Chicago: Univ. of Chicago, 1957).

[7] "Did Southern Farmers Discriminate? *Agricultural History*, XVLI, No. 2, April, 1972, pp. 325–28.

[8] For a discussion of this issue, see Robert Higgs, "Race, Tenure, and Resource Allocation in Southern Agriculture, 1910," *JEH*, XXXIII (March 1973).

[9] Richard Friedman examines educational discrimination in a forthcoming study entitled *The U.S. Discriminatory System*.

GOVERNMENT AND THE GROWTH OF THE ECONOMY

In the early days of the republic, government played a crucial role in creating a hospitable environment for economic activity. The Constitution, providing for the honoring of contracts under a system of law and order, was an essential step in protecting specific rights and obligations of private property. Equally important were certain activities of the new government (particularly those initiated by Alexander Hamilton), establishing a sound credit structure and other policies discussed in Chapter V. Such political stability and a society based on law are absolutely fundamental to the development of a market economy. But beyond the government's functions in providing the hospitable setting, how important was its active intervention in economic activity through public investment, tariffs, subsidies, land grants, and similar policies?[1]

Government involvement in economic activity

In the past thirty years, a large number of studies have shown conclusively that government intervened significantly in the American economy during the nineteenth century. In Massachusetts, government was involved in a variety of regulatory activities and a wide array of subsidies for various kinds of economic activity. Even more striking was the case of Pennsylvania, where the government invested more than

---

[1] This chapter is concerned with government subsidies and investment; it does not explore other ways by which government may affect the performance of the economy, such as public land policy (Chap. X) and monetary and fiscal policies (Chap. XIII).

$100 million in public works and where, by 1844, there were public directors on the boards of more than 150 mixed (private and public) corporations. Other studies have shown that state governments in the South were major underwriters of railroad investment before the Civil War. Of $245 million invested in southern railroads in 1860, more than 55 percent had been supplied through official public agencies. States invested more than $136 million in canals between 1815 and 1860. This was more than 73 percent of canal investment. In Missouri, more than $23 million had been pledged to public improvement by 1860. State government investments declined in the post-Civil War period. Local aid was considerable in this period, and a large number of communities and counties spent substantial sums in encouraging or subsidizing transport development, particularly the development of railroads. The federal government also outdid the states by massive intervention in the form of 131 million acres in land grants to railroads for construction of transcontinental lines. This was in addition to approximately 48 million acres that were received by the railroads as state aid.

As a result of these studies, scholars have generally concluded that such governmental activity played a major part in accelerating the growth of the American economy. In a widely quoted review article, R. A. Lively summarizes the literature on the role of government.

Taken together, the works here reviewed form a consistent report of economic endeavor in an almost unfamiliar land. There, the elected public official replaced the individual enterpriser as the key figure in the release of capitalist energy; the public treasury, rather than private saving, became the major source of venture capital; and community purpose outweighed personal ambition in the selection of large goals for local economies. "Mixed" enterprise was the customary organization for important innovations, and government everywhere undertook the role put on it by the people, that of planner, promoter, investor, and regulator.[2]

The contribution of government investment

Caution, however, is clearly necessary at this point. It is one thing to point up the involvement of government at all levels in economic activity; it is something else to attribute to it a significant share of the growth of the American economy. As yet, there has been no systematic

[2] "The American System," *The Business History Review*, XXIX, No. 1 (March 1955), 81.

work that enables us to bridge this gap.[3] Unfortunately, all too often the present ideological attitudes of scholars toward government intervention have influenced their perspective on the past. What we need is an unbiased, systematic examination of the extent to which the activity of government at all levels did, or did not, actually promote economic growth. As of this date, no such analysis has been undertaken.

Again, the hypothetical alternative is essential here. We shall have to ask ourselves: What would have happened to the economy in the absence of government investment or promotion of a particular type of economic activity? During the nineteenth century, government's share of total reproducible wealth in the United States, like the realized income from government, was always a very small percentage of either total reproducible wealth or of national income. Crude estimates for the nineteenth century suggest that in each case it was not more than 5 percent of the total.

Therefore, if government did in fact play a significant role in the economy, it must have been because its effects were larger than the simply quantitative data would assert. To state that such was the case, we must first have affirmative answers to the following theoretical issues:

1) Was the social rate of return upon investments in certain areas higher than the private rate of return? To put this in simpler language, were certain kinds of economic activity much more important and much more profitable to society as a whole (that is, in their social rate of return) than they would have been to private business firms (the private rate of return)?[4]

2) Did the government deliberately and purposefully invest in activities in which there was significant difference between the private and social rate of return? That is, such differences may well have existed, but it is quite another matter to assert that the government in fact was aware of these differences and was judicious in actually making the correct investments.

3) Was the magnitude of the social rate of return on government invest-

---

[3] A beginning in this direction was made by Harvey Segal in attempting to measure the benefits of canals in *Canals and American Economic Development* (New York: Columbia Univ., 1961), Chap. 5. A critical evaluation and a systematic attempt to estimate the benefits of the Ohio canals are contained in Roger Ransom's "Canals and Development: A Discussion of the Issues," *AER*, LIV, No. 3 (May 1964).

[4] Take a simple illustration: a railroad that costs $100 million earns $10 million annually in net income. The private rate of return is 10 percent .It also increases the income of farmers along its route, however (as a result of lower transport costs), by $10 million annually. The social rate of return is 20 percent.

ment sufficiently large to make an appreciable contribution to the economy's rate of growth?

Lacking careful objective analysis, we can only resort to some impressionistic indications of particular aspects, which require further research.

1. Clearly, there were differences between private and social rates of return in a substantial number of economic activities. How important they were is hard to say. It is probably true that the capital market was imperfect in the early nineteenth century, and therefore it would have been hard for private individuals or for companies to amass sufficient capital to undertake certain economic activities that the state inaugurated. This was particularly true in the canal era. It is widely held that state governments, in underwriting canals, made it possible to attract foreign capital into such investment.[5] Certainly there is evidence to suggest that this is in fact correct. It is also probable that in many transportation investments, returns to society as a whole were greater than they would have been to a private investor, who would have been limited in the amount of tolls or rates he could have charged on a canal or a railroad. We may therefore cautiously conclude that in some significant areas there were important differences between the private and social rates of return in the economy in the nineteenth century.

2. Did the government, in fact, realize these differences—that is, was the government a wise investor? The investment of New York State in the Erie Canal immediately comes to mind. This was a brilliant venture that yielded handsomely to society. But in the same breath, we can mention the Pennsylvania Main Line Canal, a rather spectacular and costly failure. When we assess the total investment in canals, the results are still inconclusive. Some—such as the Ohio canals, in which the state government invested substantially—may or may not have been successful ventures and worthwhile for society. Others were clear failures and indeed went bankrupt very shortly. Roger Ransom cautiously summarizes the likely result of the major canal investments (Table VIII·1, p. 100). The same pattern of success and failure typifies many of the other states' projects as well as the local underwriting of

---

[5] It is important to realize that just because state government invested or made it possible to acquire capital from the London money market, government's contribution was not "indispensable." It simply means that otherwise the interest cost would have been higher or the project would have been delayed until it appeared more profitable to private investors.

TABLE VIII · 1 GOVERNMENT INVESTMENTS IN CANALS		
State ▼	Canal ▼	Cost ($000) ▼
	I. *Probably successful:*	
N. Y.	Erie Canal	$ 7,143
N. Y.	Champlain Canal	921
N. Y.	Oswego Canal	2,512
Ohio	Ohio Canal	4,245
Pa.	Delaware Division Canal	1,543
	Total successful canals	**$ 16,364**
	II. *Probably not successful:*	
Ohio	Miami and Erie Canal	5,920
Ohio	Wahlhonding Canal	607
Ohio	Hocking Canal	975
Ohio	Wabash and Erie Canal	500
N. Y.	Black River Canal	3,157
N. Y.	Genesee Valley Canal	5,663
N. Y.	Chenango Canal	2,316
Pa.	Mainline Canal*	16,473
Pa.	5 Penn. Lateral Canals†	15,033
Ind.	Wabash Canal	6,325
Ind.	Whitewater Canal	1,400
Ill.	Illinois and Michigan	6,558
Md.	Chesapeake and Ohio‡	11,071
Va.	James and Kanawha§	10,436
	Total unsuccessful canals	**$ 86,434**
	TOTAL CANAL INVESTMENT	**$102,798**

Source: Roger Ransom, "Canals and Development: A Discussion of the Issues," *AER*, LIV, No. 2 (May 1964). 375.

*Mainline Canal cost includes railroad connections.

† The five canals were: the Susquehanna Division Canal, the French Creek Canal, Beaver Canal, the North Branch Division Canal, and the West Branch Division Canal.

‡ Private company whose stock was largely owned by Maryland, Virginia, and the United States government.

§ The $5.5 million of stock was purchased by Virginia, Richmond, and Lynchburg.

economic activity that took place in the nineteenth century. Consequently, it is not possible at this point to assert one way or another
what the outcome would look like if the necessary research were done.

3. Even if necessary research to answer the first two questions
had brought us to the conclusion that government investment was
indeed a positive contribution, we would then have to know whether
its magnitude was significant. For example, take 10 percent as the
government's percentage of gross capital formation in the nineteenth

century, and assume that the social rate of return on *all* that investment was double the rate in the private sector. If the rate of growth of gross national product was 4.5 percent per year, then the government's contribution would be 20 percent of the contribution of capital to the growth rate.

Clearly, however, capital *alone* does not account for the total *extensive* and *intensive* growth of the economy—which is what the 4.5 percent growth of GNP is measuring. That is, the 4.5 percent figure measures increased output as a result of increases *both* in *inputs* of productive factors and in *efficiency* of productive factors. Population expansion of more than 80 million during the century and resultant increase in the labor force contribute an important part of the 4.5 percent. Economies of scale that are not included would be another important contributor toward this growth rate. If, therefore, we say that capital contributed two-thirds of this rate of growth, then 20 percent of 3 percent is the government's contribution to the growth rate, or six-tenths of 1 percent per year. Even this figure assumes that none of the resources devoted to government investment would have been replaced by private investment in the absence of such government intervention. If we assume more reasonably that half of this investment would have been profitable for the private sector, then the contribution of government to the rate of growth would have been an increase in output of three-tenths of 1 percent per year. This is certainly a significant figure, but it does not bear out statements that the roles of local, state, and national government were indispensable. Since I have deliberately used figures that appear to be a substantial overstatement of the likely magnitudes, the implication is that when we have done the necessary research, the *overall* contribution of government investment in the nineteenth century will be revealed as a modest one.

Considerably more spectacular, however, was the rate of return upon specific activities.[6] Surprisingly, most of these activities appear to have received far less attention than those related to transport development. Education received the most conspicuous state and local government contributions.[7] The public school system has been an important stimulus to the growth of human capital in the United States. Similarly,

---

[6] In fact, at the end of this chapter, I deliberately picked a case with extraordinary returns.

[7] In 1870 such investment was approximately 4 percent of gross capital formation. For a discussion of the development of public education and the relative decline of private education, see Albert Fishlow, "Levels of Nineteenth-Century American Investment in Education," *JEH* (Dec. 1966), 418–36.

with the passage of the Morrill Act in 1862, the land grant college made possible a wider spread of higher education than would have occurred without it. Private education at all levels would have experienced greater expansion in the absence of public education, but it would probably have resulted in a more unequal distribution of income than actually has prevailed. What, then, was the social rate of return on education in nineteenth-century America? Very little research has been done, but our present-day impression about the importance of human capital in economic development suggests that it was important and worthy of far more attention than it has received.

MEASUREMENT OF GOVERNMENT'S CONTRIBUTION TO ECONOMIC GROWTH: RESEARCH IN AGRICULTURE

Is it possible to measure the contribution of government to the growth of output in a specific sector of the economy? The answer is clearly "yes." But instead of the impressionistic accounts that have characterized the studies in the past, we must use systematic economic analysis and empirical data to achieve any useful results. Take the case of government research in agriculture in the United States.

A recent study by John Kendrick[8] shows that productivity in agriculture increased very little between about 1900 and 1920 but thereafter rose very rapidly. Ever since 1887, with the passage of the Hatch Act, the federal government and numerous state agencies have expended substantial sums of money in agricultural research.[9] What has been the contribution of this research to the observed productivity increase—that is, the social rate of return on this investment by the government? In the past fifteen years, economists have devoted a good deal of attention to measuring it. In his *Economic Organization of Agriculture*[10] Professor Theodore Schultz presents systematic evi-

---

[8] *Productivity Trends in the United States* (Princeton, N.J.: Princeton Univ., 1961).

[9] An intriguing question is raised by the failure of productivity to expand substantially until more than thirty years after the beginning of this research.

[10] (New York: McGraw-Hill, 1953), Chap. 7. I am very much indebted to Theodore W. Schultz for discussions and encouragement relating to this section of the study. The conclusions, of course, are my own.

dence to show a high rate of return on such investments by agencies of the United States Department of Agriculture as well as by state experiment stations. Instead of the overall rate of return on research in agriculture (which Schultz estimates to be approximately 30 percent), let us take one specific (and spectacularly successful) case—

TABLE VIII · 2	HYBRID CORN: ESTIMATED RESEARCH EXPENDITURES AND NET SOCIAL RETURNS, 1910–1955 (millions of 1955 dollars)

Year ▼	Total research expenditures (private and public) ▼	Year ▼	Total research expenditures (private and public) ▼	Net social returns* ▼
1910	0.008	1933	0.584	0.3
1911	0.011	1934	0.564	1.1
1912	0.010	1935	0.593	2.9
1913	0.016	1936	0.661	8.3
1914	0.022	1937	0.664	21.2
1915	0.032	1938	0.721	39.9
1916	0.039	1939	0.846	60.3
1917	0.039	1040	1.090	81.7
1918	0.039	1041	1.100	105.3
1919	0.044	1042	1.070	124.3
1920	0.052	1943	1.390	140.4
1921	0.068	1944	1.590	158.7
1922	0.092	1945	1.600	172.6
1923	0.105	1946	1.820	184.7
1924	0.124	1947	1.660	194.3
1925	0.139	1948	1.660	203.7
1926	0.149	1949	1.840	209.8
1927	0.185	1950	2.060	209.0
1928	0.210	1951	2.110	218.7
1929	0.285	1952	2.180	226.7
1930	0.325	1953	2.030	232.1
1931	0.395	1954	2.270	234.2
1932	0.495	1955	2.790	239.1
		Annually after 1955	3.000	248.0

Source: Zvi Grilliches, "Research Costs and Social Returns: Hybrid Corn and Related Innovation," *JPE*, LXVI (Oct. 1958), 424. Reprinted by permission of The University of Chicago Press.

* Net of seed production cost but not net of research expenditures. Net social returns are zero before 1933.

the social rate of return on the development of hybrid corn in the United States.[11]

Hybrid corn yields are 15 to 20 percent higher than those of the earlier open-pollinated varieties. Using the hypothetical alternative, we may measure what the value of output would have been in the absence of hybrid corn, versus the value of output that actually existed as a result of its development. Against this value, we must charge the costs—the total costs of research and development, as well as any additional costs involved in using hybrid corn seed versus the open-pollinated varieties.[12] Table VIII·2, p. 103, presents the results. As of 1955, for a research expenditure of $3 million, the net social returns were $248 million; or to put it more simply, the social rate of return on this investment, as of 1955, was at least 700 percent.

The methods used here are similar to those of "benefit-cost analysis" which have been developed to measure the rate of return upon government investments, particularly in the field of water resources. It is clear that some kinds of returns are extremely difficult to quantify. Nevertheless, the development of this systematic method for measuring the rate of return upon government investment today points the way toward the kinds of research that are necessary to evaluate the contributions of government of yesterday.

---

[11] The following section comes from Zvi Griliches, "Research Costs and Social Returns—Hybrid and Corn Related Innovations," *JPE*, LXVI, No. 5 (Oct. 1958).

[12] I am omitting from this discussion a large number of highly complex technical issues in economics, such as the problems of present worth, the appropriate interest rate, and the assumed supply and demand elasticities.

SHIPS, RAILROADS,
AND ECONOMIC GROWTH

Improvements in transportation in the nineteenth century have occupied a central place in explaining a substantial part of the American economy's development. Steam power for land and water transportation has appeared to most economic historians as the very epitome of the Industrial Revolution extending to transportation. It is to be expected, therefore, that the steamship and the railroad should have been deemed indispensable in the expansion of international trade and in promoting the settlement and economic development of a continent.

In addition to its revolutionary role in lowering transport costs, the railroad has also been credited with still further substantial effects upon economic development. The size of investment—that is, the amount of capital invested—in railroads in the United States in the nineteenth century made it the first billion-dollar industry in this country by the time of the Civil War. Not only was it a large-scale industry; the railroad in the course of its building needed iron, steel, machinery, and timber; therefore, it was given credit for inducing expansion in still other industries. Finally, as a large-scale enterprise, the railroad required the development of sophisticated methods of large-scale business organization and has been looked upon as a pioneer in the development of corporate organization in the United States.

Impressions are no substitute for systematic analysis, however, which suggests a different interpretation of the role played by improving transportation in the nineteenth century economy. To put this role in perspective, let us carefully examine the changing costs of transportation, the investment induced by transportation enterprises, the organizational improvements effected by large-scale transportation media, and the relocation of economic activity as a result of changing transport costs.

Changing costs of transportation

Figure IX·1 gives us some notion of how ocean transportation costs fell from the early nineteenth to the early twentieth century. The black line is an index of freight rates themselves over this period; the white line shows the freight rate index divided by a price index for the period, so that we can see how the freight rates fell relative to the

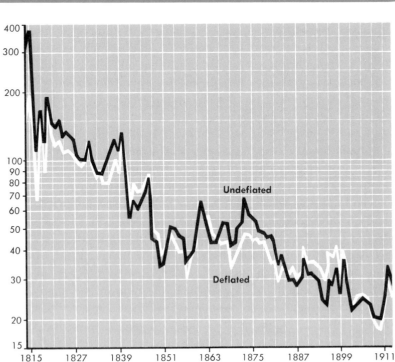

Fig. IX · 1   INDEX OF U.S. EXPORT FREIGHT RATES, 1814–1913

Source: Douglass C. North, "The Role of Transportation in the Economic Development of North America," paper presented to The International Congress of the Historical Sciences (Vienna, August 1965) and published in *Les grandes voies maritimes dans le monde XVe–XIXe siècles* (Paris, 1965).

general price level. The chart shows that the most striking fall of ocean freight rates occurred between 1815 and 1850, followed by a period in which freight rates fell very little. Then they fell somewhat more modestly in the years between 1873 and 1908.

Although the steamship substituted for the sailing ship in passenger travel as early as 1850, it did not substitute for the sailing ship in the carriage of bulk goods in ocean transportation until much later. Indeed, as late as 1880 most of the goods carried in ocean transportation were going by sail, and the changeover from sail to steam did not occur in most of the long-haul routes in the world until the very end of the nineteenth century, when the triple-expansion engine made it possible for steam to compete effectively with sail. Some routes, such as the long haul of grain from the Pacific Northwest to Liverpool, 14,000 miles around Cape Horn, were still dominated by sailing ships right up until World War I. In short, it took the steamship approximately eighty years from its inception at the beginning of the nineteenth century to replace the sailing ship in the carriage of most bulk commodities. Yet, the striking feature of the chart is that the fall in transportation rates is most rapid in a period when sail dominated ocean shipping; therefore, the reduction in cost must be attributed primarily to the sailing ship. Even after 1870, improvement in sailing-ship efficiency continued to enable the sailing vessel to compete with the steamship right up until the end of the century. Clearly, it was the sailing ship and not the steamship that was responsible in good part for the dramatic fall in ocean transportation costs in the nineteenth century.

Figure IX·2, p. 108, summarizes the fall in inland freight rates from 1784 to 1900. Since the rates in this chart are not adjusted for differences in the price level, some of the movement reflects changes in general prices rather than real falls in transportation costs themselves. The pattern of rate changes is so great, however, that such a bias does not really alter the picture very much. Here, one can see that the major decline in inland transportation rates is a result of the difference between wagon and water rates. Note that the upstream and downstream river rates and canal rates are consistently lower than railroad rates. The dramatic technological change in inland transportation was not the advent of the railroad (which is the one that we customarily think of), but rather the development of the steamship on inland waters. The consequent fall in rates for upstream river transportation after 1816 directly reflects the use of steamboats on the

Fig. IX · 2   GENERAL PATTERN OF
INLAND FREIGHT RATES, 1784–1900

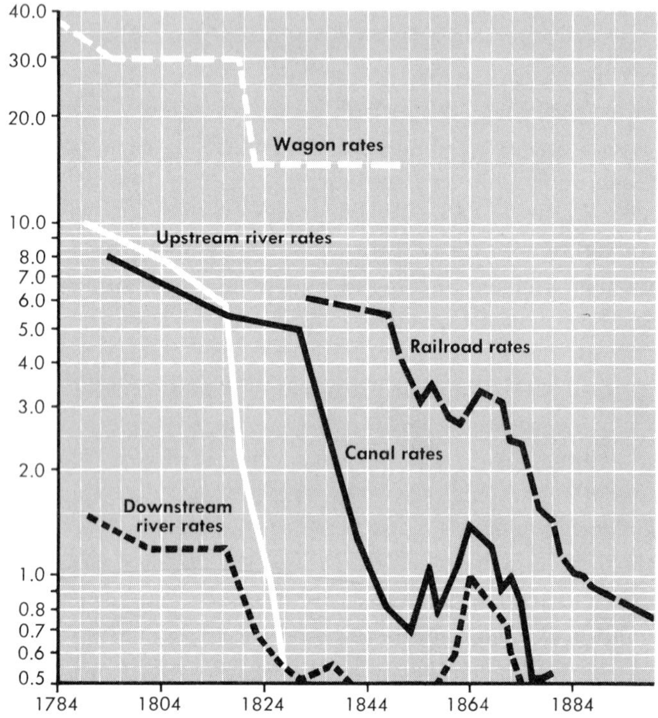

Source: North, "The Role of Transportation in the Economic Development of North America."

Mississippi River and its tributaries. Here is clearly a case of technological development playing a significant part in lowering transportation costs.

Railroad rates fell dramatically throughout the century, but as noted above, they remained higher than water rates. The railroad's domination of inland transportation during the last half of the nineteenth century, therefore, must have been due to reasons other than the direct one of simply offering lower ton-mile rates. This is the subject to be examined at the end of this chapter.

Investment induced by transportation enterprises

The expansion of the railroad into every corner of the United States in the nineteenth century was certainly a dramatic event, graphically presented by Fig. IX·3, p. 110. Increased railroad mileage gives a clue to the way in which the railroad came to dominate internal transportation, and the investment necessary to build this immense system is recorded in Table IX·1. Induced investment in other industries, however, is not necessarily a benefit to the economy, since the improved productivity has already been passed on to the consumer, in the form of lower transport rates. Investments in other kinds of enterprises—iron, steel, timber, machinery, and so forth—increase the productivity of the economy only to the extent that they make possible lower costs in those industries, costs that would not have been reduced without the railroad's demand. Since this subject has already been examined, no further discussion will be offered here.

TABLE IX·1	REAL NET CAPITAL STOCK IN RAILROADS 1838–1909 (in millions of 1909 dollars)		
End of year ▼	Equipment ▼	Track ▼	Total* ▼
1838	$ 2.9	$ 79.8	$ 82.7
1848	11.4	219.4	230.9
1858	59.2	1,000.1	1,059.2
1869	111.7	1,629.4	1,741.1
1879	286.1	3,011.2	3,297.4
1889	606.8	5,867.2	6,474.0
1899	749.6	6,811.0	7,560.6
1909	1,658.2	8,799.7	10,457.9

Source : Fishlow, "Productivity and Technological Change in the Railroad Sector, 1840–1910," p. 606
* Totals adjusted to nearest thousand.

The way to run a railroad—or a factory

A further point does need examination: the role of the railroad in the development of sophisticated large-scale organization. The railroad clearly was the first large-scale enterprise in America, the kind of enterprise that required a corporate form of organization and the solving of complex management problems. It is difficult to assess the importance of the railroad's role in this process of improved organization. One is tempted to believe that it was a dependent variable in the sense that—given the gradual development of large-scale enterprise—a learning process would inevitably have taken place, whatever the industry

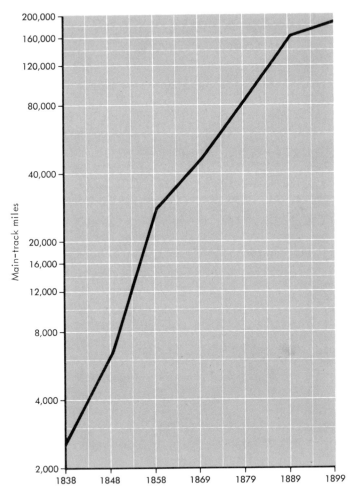

Fig. IX · 3   EXPANSION OF RAILROAD MILEAGE, 1838–1899

Source: Albert Fishlow, "Productivity and Technological Change in the Railroad Sector, 1840–1910," *Output, Employment, and Productivity in the United States after 1800* (New York: National Bureau of Economic Research, 1966), p. 596.

was. Since manufacturing was also developing large-scale organization by the end of the nineteenth century, such improvement of efficiency might very well have happened as a result of expansion in the size of the manufacturing firm.

The development and financing of the railroad in the nineteenth century was not an unmitigated gain, even if we do acknowledge that it paved the way for improvements in organization in general. Some aspects of railroad financing and organization in the United States in the nineteenth century were clearly a detriment. The financial manipulations of railroad financiers in the decades from the 1870s to 1900 are familiar history—manipulations that led to substantial watering of the stock, that is, to expansion in the amount of nominal capital without really increasing the tangible earning power of the railroad. The result was a series of titanic battles among railroad financiers, in which bondholders—and they were often British bondholders—frequently suffered at the expense of the manipulators. The activities of Drew, Fisk, and Gould in the Erie Railroad form a famous episode but not an isolated one. It was not until the very end of the century that wild railroad financing schemes came to an end. Clearly, these had involved some costs to improving organization, in the sense that they had made risks higher. American and English investors were more reluctant to invest in railroads than they would have been had the management been more responsible. Railroad finance, therefore, was sometimes a detriment to improvement of economic organization and to improvements in the capital market. The actual costs have never been ascertained; but they doubtless were of some significance, and they afford a counterweight to whatever importance attaches to the railroad as an agent in improving our knowledge about large-scale business organization.

Relocation of economic activity

Falling costs of transportation, particularly ocean transportation, show little evidence of relocating major forms of economic activity in the United States. Perhaps their greater impact was on other countries; for example, the dramatic fall in the inland and ocean transportation costs in carrying grain and other foodstuffs to Europe hastened the relative decline of European agricultural production. The development of the North Pacific grain trade from Seattle and Portland to Liverpool was a case in point. Here, a major new wheat-producing area was brought into the world market by two factors: a fall of inland transportation costs of getting wheat from the inland empire to Seattle and Portland, combined with savings effected by a more efficient ocean transportation around Cape Horn. But this is perhaps the most

TABLE IX . 2	REGIONAL EMPLOYMENT IN MANUFACTURING (percent of total U.S. mfg. employees)						
	1859 ▼	1869 ▼	1879 ▼	1889 ▼	1899 ▼	1904 ▼	1909 ▼	1914 ▼
New England	29.88	26.76	24.31	20.57	18.91	17.87	17.30	16.83
Mid. Atlantic	41.66	39.52	42.04	38.69	37.54	36.99	35.82	35.89
Great Lakes	12.09	18.36	19.19	22.29	22.65	22.29	22.73	23.73
Southeast	9.80	8.48	7.57	8.90	11.55	12.87	13.61	13.05
Plains	2.30	4.79	4.46	6.01	5.41	5.37	5.32	5.10
Southwest	0.34	0.37	0.44	0.67	0.79	0.97	1.26	1.30
Mountain	0.03	0.17	0.31	0.49	0.71	0.69	0.82	0.82
Far West	3.90[a]	1.54	1.70	2.37	2.43	2.93	3.14	3.26

[a] Including gold mining.

Source: Figures for 1859 are from U.S. Census Office, *The Eighth Census: Manufactures of the United States in 1860* (Washington: GPO, 1865). These are the raw "number of hands employed' figures and are not strictly comparable with subsequent years.

From 1869 to 1909 inclusive, figures are from Richard A. Easterlin, "Estimates of Manufacturing Activity," *Population Redistribution and Economic Growth, United States, 1870–1950*, (Philadelphia: The American Philosophical Society, 1957), I, 684. These figures have been adjusted from original census data in several ways and are rounded to the nearest hundreds.

Figures for 1914 are based on the "average wage earners" category of U.S. Census Office, *Abstract of the Census of Manufactures, 1914* (Washington: GPO, 1917). In order to make them roughly comparable to the 1869–1909 data, percentage changes from 1909 to 1914 in the census figures were calculated, and these were applied to the 1909 figures from the above source. This assumes that structural changes in employment were not great between 1909 and 1914.

dramatic case in which transportation costs by sea had an effect upon the development of a new economic activity in the United States.

To what extent was economic activity internally relocated by the railroad? Table IX·2 shows the changes over a quarter of a century (1859–1914). It is apparent that New England declined substantially and the Middle Atlantic states slightly during this period, while other areas increased their manufacturing share. The Southeast declined until 1879 and then grew substantially. The Far West grew at a later period, and the Plains states grew slightly. How much of this changing pattern of economic activity was due to the railroads? Some part of it surely was. The shift of textiles out of New England into the South probably was accounted for, at least in part, by the growth of railroad transportation in the South in later years. Some other industries were resource oriented, and the availability of the railroad made it possible for plants to be nearer their natural resources. The usefulness of some timberlands and other natural resources was certainly increased by the development of the railroad. On the other hand, it was the modifi-cation, rather than initiation, of industrial activities for which the railroad could take credit in certain areas, particularly in the Middle Atlantic and Great Lakes states. There the transportation needs were already met by water, and the railroad led, at most, to rather minor relocations of industrial activity.

It is clear that the acceleration of settlement and agricultural production in the western two-thirds of the United States was strik-ingly influenced by the advent of railroads. Maps 1 and 2, pp. 114–15, are evidence of the railroads' influence on settlement and agricultural output. Map 1 shows population density and transportation facilities in Illinois in 1850. Note that density was greatest in the peripheral counties where cheap water transportation was available (as well as along navigable waterways). In the next ten years, approximately 2,700 miles of railroad opened up the whole interior of the state, and the results are shown in Map 2. The agricultural output showed corre-spondingly striking gains.[1] The shift of the wheat industry westward into the Great Plains and the opening of new agricultural areas where transportation was available reflected the impact of railroad transporta-tion upon relocation of agriculture. Even here, however, its significance can be overstated. Robert Fogel has estimated (see below) that while less than half the land mass of the United States in 1890 was within forty miles of a navigable waterway, more than three quarters of the agricultural land was within such limits, the limits of feasible com-mercial agriculture. The great bulk of the land outside these limits was between the 100th meridian and the Sierra Nevada mountains; and as of 1890, it produced only 2 percent of the country's agricultural products.

INFLUENCE OF THE RAILROAD
ON AMERICAN ECONOMIC GROWTH

Two studies of the influence of the railroad on American eco-nomic growth have led to almost a decade of controversy. In 1964 Robert Fogel published his *Railroads in American Economic Growth*,[2]

---

[1] See Douglass C. North ,*The Economic Growth of the United States, 1790–1860* (Engle-wood Cliffs, N.J.: Prentice-Hall, 1961). pp, 146–53.

[2] (Baltimore: Johns Hopkins Univ.).

POPULATION DENSITY (BY COUNTY)

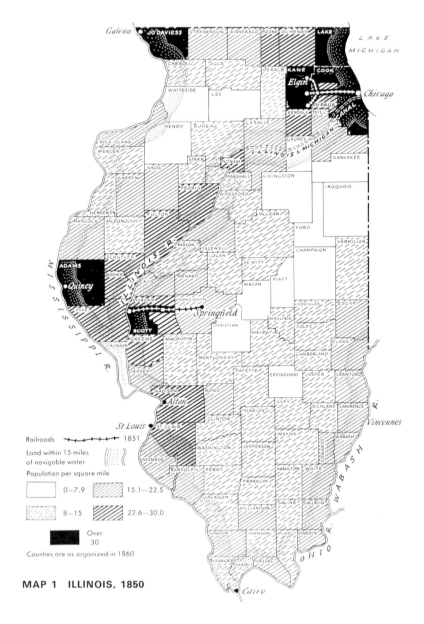

Railroads ━━┿━┿━┿━┿━ 1851

Land within 15 miles
of navigable water

Population per square mile

☐ 0—7.9   ▨ 15.1—22.5

▨ 8—15   ▨ 22.6—30.0

■ Over
30

Counties are as organized in 1860

MAP 1   ILLINOIS, 1850

Source : both maps from Douglass C. North, *The Economic Growth of the United States, 1790–1860* (Englewood Cliffs, N.J. : Prentice-Hall, 1961), pp. 147, 149.

AND TRANSPORTATION FACILITIES

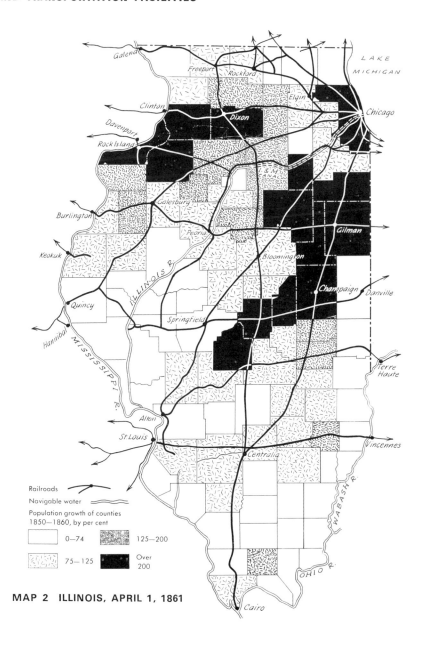

Railroads
Navigable water
Population growth of counties
1850—1860, by per cent

0—74	125—200
75—125	Over 200

MAP 2   ILLINOIS, APRIL 1, 1861

in which he estimated the social savings of the railroad in 1890 to be approximately 5 percent of gross national product. Fogel's conclusion was based upon the volume of goods moved by the railroad in 1890; he estimated the cost of moving that same volume by the next best alternative (primarily water transportation). He adjusts his conclusion for differential cargo losses and inventory costs.[3] This finding was perhaps the most controversial result of the new economic history, since it was widely at variance with the general impression of the railroad's indispensability. In 1965 Albert Fishlow published *American Railroads and the Transformation of the Ante-Bellum Economy*,[4] in which he shows a social savings of 5 percent in 1860, and any reasonable extrapolation of that figure to 1890 would lead to a figure in excess of 10 percent. The difference between the two figures stemmed not only from measuring different things (Fogel extrapolated his findings from an estimate of the costs of transporting agricultural goods) but also from a basic difference with respect to what the costs would have been in moving the goods by the next best alternative. The controversy has been endlessly discussed in the journals.[5] At stake is a basic dilemma surrounding the use of the hypothetical alternative or counterfactual proposition. The construction of a hypothetical alternative means in this case building a model of how the economy would have performed under different circumstances—namely, without railroads. This hypothetical alternative must be, in effect, a general equilibrium model that would allow for the total consequences to the economy of the absence of the railroad. Once we begin to consider the magnitude and ramifications of such an absence, it is easy to see what widely divergent results we could get. What would have happened to other transport means, to technological change, to all the industries supplying railroads?

The hypothetical alternative is obviously essential to the study of economic history, but it will hardly reduce a controversy that involves repercussive effects of the magnitude possible here. In considering the

---

[3] Fogel slights the issue that some goods (perishables, for example) could not have moved at all by alternatives, and therefore added inventory costs understate the difference. Also, he does not include passenger savings, which were substantial. See J. H. Boyd and Gary Walton, "The Social Savings from Nineteenth Century Rail Passenger Services," *EEH*, IX (Spring 1972).

[4] (Cambridge, Mass.: Harvard Univ.).

[5] See citations in Bibliography to Chapter IX. Detailed criticisms concerned whether rates measured social savings appropriately as well as exactly what is meant by social savings.

railroad, we are dealing with the major single source of investment during much of the late nineteenth century and trying to ascertain all of its consequences for 60 years. That burdens the hypothetical alternative with too many possible (and reasonable) alternative developments.

I don't mean to suggest that Fogel and Fishlow have not written enormously valuable studies. In fact, to the contrary, the studies have not only contributed a great deal to our understanding of railroad history but they have forced clarification of the exact nature of what is meant by social savings and of the limitations inherent in the use of the counterfactual proposition.

LAND POLICY AND THE
WESTWARD MOVEMENT, 1785–1890

Perhaps the most dramatic episode in American economic history is the settling and populating of our continental territory. A vast area was settled in America between 1776 and the 1890s, when the superintendent of the U.S. Census reported that the frontier had disappeared in America. At the time of the Declaration of Independence, only the eastern seaboard was settled, although some pioneers had crossed the mountains and established themselves on the other side of the Appalachian Mountains, in the Ohio Valley. Farther west, the country was for the most part unknown to white men.

Over these years the United States acquired lands in big chunks: the Louisiana Purchase, acquired from the French in 1803; Florida in 1819; and Texas, California, and the territory of Oregon in the 1840s. By 1853, with the Gadsden Purchase of a strip on the Mexican border, the contiguous territorial boundaries of the continental United States had been established.

Settling these areas was a much longer, dramatic story that begins with the expedition of Lewis and Clark. These two with their party followed the Missouri River to its headwaters, crossed the Rocky Mountains, traveled down the Columbia, and wintered at its mouth. When they returned, they told a story of an extraordinary land, full of promise—a land that was to dominate much of our history later in the century, as venturesome Americans successively looked over the new frontier and settled it. Fur traders came hard on the heels of Lewis and Clark. In fact, some members of their expedition turned right around and went back upriver to search for beaver pelts. Following the fur trader came the farmer and the miner, and cities developed as the frontier receded westward. The center of population continued to move west as this immense expanse of territory was settled and developed in the nineteenth century.

Public land policy: description

Geographical expansion has been an exciting story that has preoccupied our attention. It has also presented extraordinary economic problems, beginning in the 1780s, when the federal government was permitted to gain title to land west of the Appalachians, originally claimed by the individual states. An important decision early in the history of this nation was that these lands would not be retained by the government but would be transferred to private ownership.

This point decided, the government had a number of different and sometimes contradictory objectives that could be reached by the sale of public lands. Its prime objective was to aid the settlement of the United States and to create conditions that would favor economic development. But it also wanted to raise revenue; and public land sales proved to be a major, although very irregular, source of revenue for a long period in our history.

There was a variety of possible methods for making these lands available to the public, and their disposal has become one of the most controversial subjects in American history. A look at Table X·1 shows how public land sales changed between 1785 and 1832 as a result of changes in congressional legislation.

TABLE X · 1   MAJOR ACTS AFFECTING LAND DISTRIBUTION, 1785–1832

Act	Minimum unit in acres	Minimum auction price per acre	Terms of sale
1785	640	$1.00	Cash, ½ by township; ½ by sections
1796	640	2.00	½ cash, ½ credit for 1 yr.
1800	320	2.00	¼ cash; ¼ in 2 yrs.; ¼ in 3 yrs.; ¼ in 4 yrs.
1804	160	2.00	Same as in 1800
1820	80	1.25	Cash
1832	40	1.25	Cash

Source: Philip H. Overmeyer, "Westward Expansion Before the Homestead Act," in *Growth of the American Economy* (2nd ed.), ed. Harold F. Williamson (Englewood Cliffs, N.J.: Prentice-Hall 1951), p. 104.

The first act, in 1785, not only set minimum acreage and price, but also laid out the whole "township" system of division that has characterized American surveying ever since. Less durable were the minimum standards. These shifted drastically, as the table indicates; they dropped from 640 acres in 1875 to 40 acres in 1832. The minimum price per acre, meantime, started at $1.00, went to $2.00 until 1804, and then dropped to $1.25 between 1820 and 1832. The terms, cash or credit, varied. The general system of distribution was to put the lands up for auction. If no one bid above the set minimum, the land remained unsold.

Ever since the Revolution, the government has given away substantial tracts. Veterans of wars received military bounty warrants entitling them to land; and as large numbers of these warrants accumulated from earlier wars, they came to be traded actively, so that they were bought and sold like any other valuable claim. As noted in previous chapters, both the federal government and the states gave public lands to the railroads to encourage the building of transcontinental systems. A total of 180 million acres went toward this objective, the Northern Pacific receiving the lion's share but other lines also benefiting greatly.

In 1841, the Pre-emption Act was put into effect to protect squatters, those eager settlers who had gone out ahead of the surveyors and, holding no title to their land, found themselves faced with eviction, sometimes by government troops. The new act gave squatters first rights to purchase their land if they had settled on it before the survey. In 1854 a Graduation Act was passed. Lands that had not sold at the government minimum were now permitted to be sold at lower prices. Then came the landmark enactment that has frequently been considered a watershed in the history of America's public lands—the Homestead Act. This act, in 1862, stipulated that a bona fide settler could receive title to 160 acres free and clear (or 320 acres if he were married) provided that he lived on the land or cultivated it for five years. As time went on, it became clear that additional acts were needed, particularly in areas where mining and lumbering were involved, and this led to the Timber Culture Act in 1873, the Desert Act of 1877, and the Timber Cutting Act and Timber and Stone Act of 1878.[1]

---

[1] These acts were designed to encourage tree growing, to aid in settlement and irrigation of desert areas, and to dispose of timber lands.

Public land policy: criticism

This long history of legislation delineating the government's position on public land sales has been the target of endless invective. In general, historians have been extremely critical of the whole system, feeling that it rewarded greed and speculation. There is no doubt that speculation in public lands was a favorite occupation of Americans in the nineteenth century. Not only big speculators bought vast tracts of land ahead of settlement and attempted to sell them as settlers moved west, but smaller holders speculated, too. Many a farmer bought more land than he could possibly cultivate, with the idea of holding it for a rise in value. As a result, speculation is blamed for discouraging actual farming and encouraging the view of land as a speculative commodity. It is also alleged that the westward movement was impaired by the system of land disposal that left large tracts of land unsettled for a long time, either because the minimum price was too high or because speculators were holding the land off the market for a higher price. Critics also contend that the economic growth of the country was hampered by this disposition of land, partly because of the inhibition of settlement that resulted from holding land off the market and partly from the fact that the land acts were not well-suited to the particular needs of the times—that is, in the early period of rich lands, large tracts were specified as a minimum; but in the later period, when nonarable pasture characterized the available land, the maximum size under the Homestead Act was far too small for an efficient farm unit.

Also, historians have asserted that the national distribution of wealth was adversely affected by the way that lands were given away: monopolists, speculators, and the rich were favored at the expense of the hardworking farmer and the poor settler. It is a generally held view that one aim in the disposal of public lands should have been to assure that the wage earner and the poor in the East had a safety valve, a way to escape the city and poverty. Before re-examining these criticisms in more detail, it will be helpful to take an economist's-eye view of the whole process of the westward movement. In part, it was simply people moving to escape the urban life, the life of settlements; venturesome people wanted to go out into the wilds; some (like the Mormons) wanted to escape religious persecution. But escape was only a part of the motive force in westward movement. The typical pattern of settlement was guided by economic motives—people went west because they felt that they could better themselves economically, in light of America's burgeoning demand for agricultural goods, minerals, and lumber. As population grew and the demand for such products increased, particularly for crops to feed the industrializing and urbanizing East, the West offered improving opportunity to supply this demand.

We are familiar with the way in which a market economy, through price changes, automatically signals such demands. In this case, the demand was not only from the expanding East, but from foreigners as well. Before the Civil War, cotton was the leading export. Wheat had come into prominence as an export at the time of the Irish Famine in the 1840s and gained great momentum after the war. Ample lands were available for agricultural expansion; the limiting factor was transportation, but we have already traced the way this constraint was loosened. Canals and waterways in the eastern half of the United States provided an effective medium for carrying goods interregionally to market; then the railroad entered the plains and the prairies, providing transportation where no effective waterway existed. To balance the scales for westward settlement, then, it is evident that on the one hand people were influenced by the growing demand for farm goods, lumber, and minerals; on the supply side, transportation improvements were opening up new areas to make greater production possible. These developments should be reflected in price movements, and that is exactly where they do show up. Surges of movement into new lands occurred, from 1816 to 1818, in the 1830s, the 1850s, the late 1860s, and in the 1880s. Each of these surges was induced by a rapidly expanding demand that produced rising prices of agricultural goods.[2] It is well to keep this in mind, because the decisiveness of such market influences is not included in many descriptions of westward settlement. The view that the West not only dominated our history but that it was a refuge in bad times for the poor and unemployed is simply untenable. The unemployed and the poor in general did not have the means to go west and start farming. Moreover, most people moved west in good times, in periods of rising prices, of expanding demand, when the prospects for making money from this new land looked brightest; and this aspect characterized the whole pattern of settlement.

If the foregoing summary of historians' criticisms has suggested that they agree upon the inadequacies of the country's public land

---

[2] A fall in transport costs or *any improvement* in the prospective income of the farmer would produce these results.

policy, a warning must be issued. In fact, as the following quotations from leading authorities indicate, the subject is in a state of substantial confusion.

Homeseekers in the West, being unwilling to go far afield from means of transportation or to settle upon the inferior lands remaining open to homestead, and lacking capital with which to purchase farms and to provide equipment for them, were frequently forced to become tenants on the lands of speculators. Thus farm tenancy developed in the frontier stage at least a generation before it would have appeared had the homestead system worked properly.[3]

In fact, however, the government steadily offered more land than the market could absorb at the minimum price, and the auction system soon became a joke. So much first-class land was offered that bids never rose much above the minimum, speculative buying was encouraged, a lot of land remained unsold, and so far as any settlement followed sale, it was scattered among tracts of idle land in public or in speculative hands.[4]

When newly surveyed lands were first announced for sale, the squatters had to arrange for the purchase of their lands—made valuable by their improvements—before the opening of the auction, or run the risk of losing them to speculators.[5]

The theoretical defense of pre-emption was that the squatters were public beneficiaries engaged in actual development of the West. Exposing to public auction the tracts they had improved would permit others to confiscate the fixed improvements by purchasing the fee in the land. The defect in this theory is that the alleged improvements were generally negligible in value if not altogether invisible.[6]

How significant was the Homestead Law in enabling settlers to acquire land and to establish themselves on going farms? It is clear that it was most successful in the period from 1863 to 1880 when the greater proportion of homesteads were being established in the states bordering on the Mississippi River. It was successful also in parts of Kansas and Nebraska well east of the 98th meridian where there was abundance of rain, and where commutations, relinquishments, and abandonments were fewer than they were to be in other areas later. In these eighteen years, homesteaders filed on 469,000 tracts and by 1885 had made their final entries and were in

[3] Paul Wallace Gates, "The Homestead Law in an Incongruous Land System," *AHR*, XLI, No. 4 (July 1936), 670.

[4] Thomas LeDuc, "History and Appraisal of U.S. Land Policy to 1862," *Land Use Policy and Problems in the United States*, ed. Howard W. Ottoson (Lincoln: Univ. of Nebraska, 1963), p. 5.

[5] Paul Wallace Gates, "The Role of the Land Speculator in Western Development," *Pennsylvania Magazine of History and Biography*, LXVI, No. 3 (July 1942); reprinted in *The Public Lands*, ed. Vernon Carstensen, (Madison: Univ. of Wisconsin, 1963), p. 356.

[6] LeDuc, "History and Appraisal of U.S. Land Policy to 1862," p. 12.

process of getting title on 55 percent. Doubtless some would complete their residence requirements in later years.[7]

The land-use pattern of the twenty-nine public land states of the South, the Middle West, and the Far West is the result of a long process of development and adaptation in which such factors as speculation, absentee ownership, credit usury, farm mechanization, transportation, and government controls have played important roles. Only recently has the United States come to realize the monstrous errors it permitted to develop in this land-use pattern. Likewise, only recently has it become apparent that this pattern is the product in part of mistaken land policies which were once thought to be establishing a democratic system of landownership.[8]

These quotations do more than simply show the contradictions that riddle the interpretive positions on the subject. They point up the inability of the historian to come to grips with the problems without the systematic use of theory to examine the issues and without the testing of resultant hypotheses by careful empirical research. I do not mean to suggest that any quotation is not founded upon some detailed story of the vast panorama of settlement of the public domains, because no doubt each has a factual basis. And this very fact reflects the immensely rich and variegated story of the westward movement. But from these particular stories the historian has generalized the consequences of the entire set of public land policies. It would be possible to accumulate an endless number of such stories, but they do not add up to an overall appraisal of the policies. If we are to assert that the policies adversely affected economic growth, then we must assess them in their relation to the determinants of economic growth; or if we are to assess their effects upon welfare or equity, we must conduct a careful examination of the consequences of the policies on the distribution of income.

EFFECT OF PUBLIC LAND POLICIES ON GROWTH AND WELFARE IN THE NINETEENTH CENTURY

Since preliminary spadework has not been done, conclusions must be limited; but at least we can precisely define the issues, suggest some hypotheses that must be tested, and explore the existing systematic evidence that might bear upon these hypotheses.

---

[7] Paul Wallace Gates, in *Land Use Policy and Problems in the United States*, ed. Howard W. Ottoson (Lincoln: Univ. of Nebraska, 1963) p. 41.

[8] Gates, in *The Public Lands*, p. 349.

Examination of public land policies to determine their effect on growth and welfare in the nineteenth century is complicated by (1) the number and variety of laws related to public land policies, (2) the wide variety of land and other resources that was exploited in the course of the westward movement, (3) the poor administration of public land policies, and (4) the graft and corruption that permeated the disposition of the public domain.

Continuous repetition of the words "speculator" and "land monopolization" throughout the writing on the subject requires precise examination of these terms before we can go further. Just what constitutes speculation? When anyone buys an asset with a resale or rental value, he is indulging in speculation. Buying that asset, he forgoes buying other assets, all offering prospective income streams that he takes into account. He is guessing about the future value of that asset. In contemplating the purchase of a fixed-yield bond, for example, he speculates not only that he will get the specified return, but he also guesses whether the general level of prices will rise or fall and thereby alter the real value of the fixed money return. Speculation is endemic in any private property system. It is therefore hard to imagine any way that one could dispose of public lands without speculation. Moreover, the speculator performs the important function of bearing risks in a market economy and of improving knowledge about the available alternative opportunities, thereby making the market work more perfectly.

The term "land monopolist" is simply a misuse of "monopolist." There is no meaningful sense in which a monopoly of land existed at any time in the nineteenth century. In fact, availability is the one clearly evident characteristic of the opening up of the public domain. There were immense amounts of land continuously available from a large number of different sources. People who wanted land of any quality could always get it from a host of sellers in addition to the government. That large blocks of land were at times held by single individuals is in no sense an indication of land monopoly, unless the holders actually owned such an appreciable percentage of all available land that they could influence its overall price—and this never happened in America.

Examining these salient features of public land policy in the context of the determinants of economic growth, we might, on the face of it, expect them to have very little effect upon economic growth. While a system of land distribution by auction or by giving it away (under the Homestead Act) would certainly have consequences for the distribution of income, it is not obvious that such policies would have any striking effects upon the growth of the economy. These methods of distribution generally lead to efficient resource allocation.[9] This statement perhaps begs the issue, because the historian's implicit or explicit criticisms have been that some hypothetical alternative would have yielded a higher rate of growth. However, I know of no hypothetical alternatives, either explicitly advanced by historians or implicit in their criticisms, that would produce such a result.

One explicit hypothetical alternative that has been advanced is based on the contention that the unlimited amounts of land made available had adverse effects upon economic growth. Actually, just the reverse is true. To limit the available land would have been to decrease the supply of productive factors; and since the productive factor withheld would have been land of superior quality, compared to that in production, any restriction would have had an adverse effect on the growth of the economy.

If speculators deliberately held land out of production (which should have had an adverse effect upon growth for the reasons just described), it would be surprising. The purpose of speculation is to make money, and by following a withholding policy, the speculator would have been doing just the reverse. That is, to the extent that speculators bought up great tracts of land and held them for appreciation, they were tying up large sums of money in the initial cost of acquiring the land and were foregoing the income from using that money in another way—such as buying bonds. It would have been to their advantage, while holding the land, to rent it out, but buyers were easier to find than tenants. With so much land available free or at very low prices, a settler had an opportunity for a windfall in acquiring land of his own rather than renting.

Land grants to railroads probably accelerated economic growth. First, railroad construction was consistent with improving the rate of growth. Second, this construction would have been slower, or in some cases perhaps lacking, without the land grants, because the expected private rate of return from railroad building was in some cases too low

---

[9] The exceptions to this statement are discussed farther on in this section, but the general conclusion is that a rather broad range of disposal policies, from the auction system to giving land away, was consistent with a high rate of growth. Imposing a high minimum price, however, would have had adverse effects, for reasons discussed above.

to encourage investors to put their funds to this use. Third, the land grants gave impetus to construction by permitting investors to share, through the appreciation of land values, in some of the otherwise uncapturable returns from railroad building.

Public land policies had few adverse effects on economic growth, none of them very significant; but four might be mentioned. One, giving away land under the Homestead Act probably encouraged some inefficiency by attracting to agriculture people who would have been more productive in other employments. Two, until the Graduation Act, large parcels of land were left idle because the capitalized expected income stream from them was lower than the minimum price set by the government. Clearly, the Graduation Act should have come earlier, so that these lands could sooner have been put to productive use. Three, the unit of 160 acres set by the Homestead Act became increasingly inappropriate as available land dwindled to nonarable pasture land for which any efficient use would require much larger tracts. Admittedly, the ultimate result of this would be gradual consolidation into larger parcels of land as settlers recognized the facts; in the short run, however, and with the settlers' imperfect knowledge of farming possibilities, it probably led to poor utilization of the land. Four, the alternate sections in railroad land grant areas—that is, those sections retained by the government for sale at auction—were held off the market for varying periods of time. It would have augmented national income had these lands been sold more rapidly, since they were located where the potential income was greatly enhanced by availability of lower cost transportation.

The broad, tentative conclusion to be drawn, therefore, is that subject to the exceptions just noted, land policies in general were consistent with a high rate of economic growth, and it would be hard to develop a hypothetical alternative that would be a very great improvement. These conclusions follow, however, only if the tentative hypotheses advanced above withstand empirical tests, and very little systematic work has given us evidence for testing. Robert Fogel's *The Union Pacific Railroad: A Case in Premature Enterprise*[10] shows that the social rate of return on one land grant railroad, the Union Pacific, was extremely high and substantially higher than the private rate of return. In the years 1870 to 1879 the private rate of

---

[10] (Baltimore: Johns Hopkins Univ., 1960).

return was 11.6 percent. The social rate of return, which includes benefits not captured by the builders (some of which are reflected in rising land values near the railroad), was 29.9 percent for these years.[11] More recently, Lloyd Mercer has computed private and social rates of return on the Central Pacific. Mercer's analysis goes beyond Fogel's: he calculates the private rate of return with and without the land grant and works out a return over the life of the project (rather than an average for a decade in the middle of the life of the investment). The results he reaches for the Central Pacific are 12.9 percent for the private return without the land grant, 14.1 percent with the land grant, and 28.5 percent as the social rate of return.[12] Clearly, in this case the social rate of return indicates that the railroad construction contributed to economic growth, and the land grants helped to increase the private rate of return to make construction appear worthwhile to the private builders.

The major effect of public land policies was upon the distribution of wealth. Did they, as so many historians say, favor the rich at the expense of the poor? Without the necessary evidence, the following conclusions are tentative. First of all, giving away the land instead of selling it is a redistribution of income in favor of the homesteader and against the taxpayer (rich and poor): the government must get revenue from sources other than land sales, and the homesteader is getting a windfall in free land that has a positive value. Next, it is probable that large speculators did better than small ones. They were better informed, had better knowledge of the complex laws governing land disposal, had better knowledge of the possible alternatives, and —in a somewhat imperfect capital market—had better access to capital than the small speculator had. We would expect, therefore, that their rate of return on investment in land would typically have been higher than that of the small speculator or of the individual settler.

To the best of my knowledge, there have been no significant studies of the land disposal system's impact upon income distribution, exploring the rate of return received by large speculators compared to those of small speculators or settlers, nor has any examination of land grants to the railroads disclosed their effects on income distribu-

---

[11] *Ibid.*, pp. 96–103.

[12] Lloyd Mercer, "Land Grants to American Railroads: Social Cost or Social Benefit," *The Business History Review*, XLIII, No. 2 (Summer 1969), p. 142. Also see his "Rate of Return for Land Grant Railroads: The Central Pacific System," *JEH*, XXX (September 1970).

tion.[13] If we had this information, we could compare it with the hypothetical alternative—which would be a system based on policies proposed by land reformers throughout the nineteenth century and implicit in many of the criticisms advanced by historians. The needed work is still to be done.

[13] A careful study by Allan and Margaret Bogue, "Profits and the Frontier Land Speculator," *JEH*, XVII (March 1957), shows a widely varied pattern in which some cases of relatively high rates of return were matched by other cases of low or negative returns, so that the general pattern does not appear to be one in which speculator profits were extremely high. It does not answer the question posed here, however, of the differential return of large versus small speculators. See also R. P. Sweringa, *Pioneers and Profits: Land Speculation on the Iowa Frontier* (Ames: Iowa State.Univ., 1968).

XI

AGRARIAN DISCONTENT—
THE PLIGHT OF THE FARMER, 1865–1900

Between the end of the Civil War and 1900, the agrarian sector
of the economy was in a continuous state of turmoil and political
unrest. A whole series of protest organizations and political parties
evolved with the aim of improving the lot of the farmer, beginning in
1867 with the Granger Movement, which aimed at a variety of economic policies including railroad regulation and the formation of
cooperatives. This was followed by the Greenback Movement, which
focused on increased circulation of paper money as a means of raising
the price level. Then came the Farmers' Alliances and the Populist
Party of the 1880s and 1890s, with a variety of reform programs culmi-
nating in a demand for free coinage of silver as well as gold. In distress, the farmer was attempting to initiate fundamental reforms in
the American economy. While the movements varied in intensity over
time and among the separate agricultural regions, they mirrored the
farmers' widespread dissatisfaction with their lot. From their viewpoint, economic issues were central to the problems they faced. But
was this view accurate? Let us look carefully.[1]

The farmers' complaints examined

The major complaints of farmers at that time, generally echoed by
modern historians, were as follows: (1) The prices of agricultural
goods had fallen more than the prices of other goods, and they had
done so because other prices had been held up by monopolistic elements in the economy. The purchasing power of the farmer, therefore,
was falling. For every bushel of wheat that he sold, he was able to
buy less of the things he demanded. (2) Railroads, grain elevator

[1] I am indebted to Ray Lindstrom, whose paper on this subject presented in a senior class
in economic history drew my attention to the material on mortgages in the Eleventh Census,
and to my colleagues Bob Thomas and Bob Higgs for our discussions of the problems.

operators, and middlemen in general were using monopolistic practices to absorb all the profits from agriculture, rather than passing on to the farmer any of the gains accruing from improving transportation and improving organization of the agricultural market. (3) The usurious rates of moneylenders were robbing the farmer. This was a complex complaint. The farmer—and subsequent historians—felt that the eastern capitalist and his western equivalent in mortgage companies were deliberately, by monopolistic practices, charging very high rates for loans to farmers, imposing a particularly heavy burden in a period of expansion when most farmers demanded such loans. Moreover, in a period of falling prices, having a fixed debt was an even heavier burden, because the dollars to be paid back were worth more at the time of repayment than they had been when the debt was contracted.

Let us examine each of these complaints in turn. First, the question of relative prices: here, a comparison of the prices of farm commodities with those of all commodities in the Warren-Pearson index fails to support the farmers' position. Figure XI·1 shows the ratio of farm prices to all prices (the agricultural terms of trade). While there

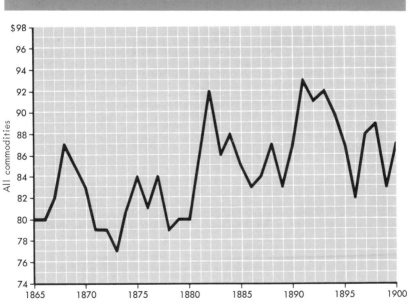

Fig. XI · 1   AGRICULTURAL TERMS OF TRADE, 1865–1900

WHOLESALE PRICES OF FARM PRODUCTS RELATIVE TO THOSE OF ALL COMMODITIES

Source: George F. Warren and Frank A. Pearson, Prices (New York: Wiley, 1933), p. 26.

are real limitations in using the Warren-Pearson index—since it measures prices at New York, Cincinnati, and Chicago rather than the prices paid and received by farmers—it is the generally accepted measure. The results show an approximately horizontal trend over the whole period. Furthermore, while the quality of farm products changed very little (if at all), that of manufactured goods was steadily improving (which is not reflected in that price index). The farmer, therefore, was really getting more for his money.

Next, consider the question of railroad rates. The traditional evidence suggests that railroad rates fell more rapidly than other prices.[2] However, recent research by Robert Higgs casts doubts on this proposition. Higgs concludes that a proper index of prices received by farmers for the major crops (corn, cotton, and wheat) relative to railroad rates shows an approximately horizontal trend until the early 1890s. Between 1893 and 1896 it moves sharply against the farmer. After 1896 there is real improvement in the farmer's position.[3] However, a look at the spread between the Liverpool price and the price on the farm shows that over this whole period the divergence narrows strikingly; the farmer was now receiving an increasing proportion of the total Liverpool sale price of a bushel of wheat. This is not surprising when we remember how much ocean freight rates fell during this period. Since the ocean freight rate on what in 1900 was less than one-third the 1870 rate, clearly the farmer's percentage of the Liverpool price had undergone dramatic improvement. Morton Rothstein summarizes the efficiency of the U.S. international grain trade as follows:

With all its imperfections, it was the highly developed and tightly organized grain business, along with additional advantages in transportation, that accounted in large measure for the unique position of the American wheat trade in the last three decades of the nineteenth century. This is less valid for the important Pacific Coast trade, where there were no elevators and transport facilities were often comparatively poor. But east of the Rockies the business of assembling, handling, financing, and transporting grain was vastly superior to that of any other nation. Once American supremacy had been established, other countries sent a stream of official and quasi-official missions to the United States to study the operation of the grain trade in the hope of emulating its efficiency. In most cases they sought to introduce

---

[2] For a summary description of railroad rate falls, see Fred Shannon, *The Farmers' Last Frontier* (New York: Holt, 1963), pp. 296–97.

[3] Robert Higgs, "Railroad Rates and the Populist Uprising," *Agricultural History*, XLIV, (July 1970).

the technology involved—such as grain elevators and systems of grading and inspection—but were anxious to forego the establishment of futures markets. Yet futures trading, which was introduced into the grain trade by Americans and reached its highest development in the United States, was fundamental to the system as a whole. In spite of the almost universal condemnation of grain speculators it was this group which reduced many of the risks inherent in a free market. On the whole they endured heavy losses down to 1896 and made relatively modest gains from the rise in prices after 1897. By protecting millers, dealers, and exporters from losses, they helped to narrow the difference between the average price paid to farmers and the average price charged to the ultimate consumer.[4]

Next, let us take a look at the mortgage picture. A surprising feature is the small percentage of mortgaged farms in the U.S. as a whole. Approximately 29 percent of the farms were mortgaged to 35 percent of their value. For the North Central area as a whole, where the complaints of the Populists were most vociferous, 38.7 percent of the farms were mortgaged in 1890. The highest states were Kansas, with 60 percent, and Nebraska, with 54 percent.[5] Equally striking is the short life span of mortgages. The average life of a farm mortgage in 1890 was four and one-half years for the North Central area, while those of Kansas and Nebraska were 3.6 and 3.7 years respectively.[6] Since the mortgages were so short that no substantial changes occurred in the price level over those brief periods of time, a falling price level with a fixed mortgage generally imposed no great hardship on the farmer; and when he took out a new mortgage, he did so at a new rate. However, there were several five-year periods when prices fell enough to cause some hardship.

The one place where there is some support for the farmer's position is in a comparison of mortgage interest rates in the North

---

[4] Morton Rothstein, "America in the International Rivalry for the British Wheat Market, 1860–1914," *The Mississippi Valley Historical Review*, XLVII (Dec. 1960). For further statistical support see Holbrook Working, "The Financial Results of Speculative Holding of Wheat," *Wheat Studies of the Food Research Institute*, VII (July 1931), 405–38. On the narrowing of the difference in prices see Henrietta Larson, "Wheat Farmer and Market in Minnesota, 1858–1900," *Studies in History, Economics, and Public Law* (New York: Columbia Univ., 1926), CXXII, 243–56; and J. Chester Bowen, *Wheat and Flour Prices from Farmer to Consumer*, U.S. Dept. Labor, Bureau of Labor Statistics, Bulletin No. 130 (Washington, 1913), *Passim*.

[5] "Real Estate Mortgages," *Eleventh Census of the U.S., 1890*, p. 123 (Percentage of Farms Mortgaged).

[6] *Ibid.*, p. 109 (Life Span of Farm Mortgages).

Central area with those in the rest of the United States. The average rate of interest was approximately 8½ percent for Kansas and Nebraska, and about 8 percent for the North Central area as a whole, compared to 5½ percent for the Atlantic area. While mortgage rates had fallen from as high as 10 or 12 percent or even more in the North Central area at an earlier date, it is likely that the capital market was still somewhat imperfect and that this imperfection worked against the western farmer in the sense that he did not enjoy as favorable rates of interest on mortgage loans as did the eastern farmer.[7] However, even within the North Central region the efficiency of the mortgage market varied. There were substantial differences between eastern and central Kansas. Bogue argues that there was real competition in the mortgage market in Iowa, Illinois, Kansas, Nebraska, and Texas.[8]

These economic complaints do not appear to have been the fundamental causes of farm distress. True, plenty of individual grievances were caused by monopoly power of the railroads, or by middlemen, or by imperfections in the capital market that allowed farm mortgage rates to be higher than elsewhere. *But had these specific situations been changed or modified anywhere along the line, the basic distress felt by the farmer would not have been alleviated.*

The sources of agrarian unrest

Its causes lay deeper. What was fundamentally at stake in the farmer's discontent was, first of all, that he found himself competing in a world market in which fluctuations in prices created great uncertainty. The bottom might drop out of his income because of a bumper crop at the other side of the world—in Argentina or Australia. When he suffered from a period of drought and poor crops, the higher prices he had learned to expect in such a case still might not be forthcoming (if other areas had a good crop year).

Let us examine in more detail what was happening to the agricultural sector during this period. First, the demand for major agricul-

---

[7] These come from *Eleventh Census of the U.S., 1890,* "Real Estate Mortgages," p. 259. Lance E. Davis makes a case for an imperfect capital market in "The Investment Market, 1870–1914: The Evolution of a National Market," *JEH,* XXV (Sept. 1965); however, it is hard to know how much of this was the increased risk of mortgages on the frontier (see quotations in previous chapter) compared to loans on farms in the East.

[8] See A. Bogue, *Money at Interest* (Ithaca, N.Y.: Cornell Univ., 1965).

tural goods, particularly wheat, cotton, corn, and livestock, had been growing rapidly. In general, it is true that increasing demand for agricultural goods is based primarily on expanding population; therefore as the United States population grew, the demand for foodstuffs also grew rapidly. This domestic increase in demand was accompanied by a growing worldwide demand for agricultural goods, which the American economy was well situated to meet. Before the Civil War, the United States had been a major supplier of cotton and, sporadically, of wheat. But with the repeal of England's Corn Laws in the middle of the nineteenth century and with its increasing industrialization, England became a major importer of wheat, and the United States became a major supplier of wheat for Britain and other European countries. Corn was primarily used to feed livestock; but livestock itself was in demand internationally, while cotton continued to be a leading American export. Thus, it is obvious that the international market formed an important component of the growing demand for American agriculture. On the supply side, as already observed in the previous chapter, the westward movement opened up new land, and the development of transport media encouraged settlers to move into these areas in response to high expected rates of return. Thus, the vast western half of America was settled.

This is not the whole story of the supply–demand relationship, however. Concurrent with the westward movement in America and the consequent rapid increase in the supply of agricultural products, particularly of wheat, other vast areas in the world were also becoming leading suppliers. Australia, Argentina, South Africa, the Ukraine of Russia, and even (for a while) India were all areas where a supply of wheat was evolving for the world market. In this competitive situation, nothing could prevent the price of agricultural commodities from fluctuating widely under varying conditions of climate and rainfall. A year of poor crops in the United States might coincide with bumper harvests in Australia, Argentina, and other parts of the world. As a result, the price of wheat would be depressed by the large quantity supplied, even though the share from western America was small. Similarly, it would be possible for the price to rise even with a bumper harvest in America if poor yields were obtained in other parts of the world. While the international market determined prices of wheat, cotton, and some other agricultural commodities, many other agricultural foodstuffs and raw materials were limited to the U.S. market.

The vast domestic market was also subject to sharp variations in supply and price.

Agriculture labors under another difficulty. In the long run, it tends to produce only moderate returns, because of the ease of entry. High prices induced a rapid expansion of agriculture and an increase in supply as people moved to new lands. But the resultant expansion tended to decrease prices so that returns fell, until readjustment took place and marginal producers moved out of that sector into more profitable occupations. This point needs to be stressed: a competitive industry is one in which an adjustment is accomplished by producers readily moving into the industry when expected returns are high and moving out of the industry when expected returns are low. Obviously, agriculture meets this definition.[9] So it is far from surprising that in the last half of the nineteenth century, with surges of new farmers moving into the industry and a vast expansion of acreage under cultivation, lengthy periods of depressed prices resulted. During such periods, prices were so low that many farmers were unable to earn the normal rate of return.

In short, a vast process of worldwide adjustment was taking place in which the demand for agricultural commodities was growing rapidly, but the supply was growing in vast surges. Inevitably, there were times of high prices and above-normal returns countered by other times of very low prices and returns. When low yields resulted from poor rainfall or other natural conditions in an area, the outcome could be still more catastrophic, coupling a low yield to lower prices. Aggravating the difficulties caused by wide fluctuations in the prices of agricultural commodities was the fact that prices in general were falling. This worldwide price decline resulted from a market economy's self-adjustment to two current factors: on the one hand, aggregate output was expanding at a rapid pace; on the other hand, the money supply of the world, based on the amount of gold available, grew more slowly. More products competing for the same amount of money resulted in a steady fall in prices. Declining prices, as discussed above, imposed an additional burden on debtor farmers who had not anticipated the decline.

As though these woes were not enough for the nineteenth-century farmer, this was the era when he was becoming a minority in America.

---

[9] Although producers move into agriculture in periods of high prices, they do not as readily move out in periods of low prices, and the lag in response (while less critical in the nineteenth century when demand was increasing rapidly) became a critical factor in the twentieth century.

Throughout all of our earlier history, his had been a dominant voice in politics and in an essentially rural society. Now, he was being dispossessed by the growing industrial might of America and its rapid urbanization. The farmer keenly felt his deteriorating status. His reading matter was full of warnings and complaints against the evils and moral decay of the city and its malign influence over the countryside. His disenchantment was an inevitable component of the vast and complex socioeconomic phenomenon that was taking place, involving both the commercialization of agriculture on a vast scale in a worldwide market and the farmers' becoming increasingly a minority group in American society.

WHAT HAPPENED TO FARM INCOME, 1865–1914

We lack good income statistics that would enable us to say with certainty what happened to farm income during the time of acute discontent from 1865 to 1896. The conclusion has often been that this was a period of continuous farmer distress resulting from falling farm income, but some of the evidence advanced above suggests that this was not likely. Yet, the period does contrast in striking fashion with the era 1896–1914, when there was evident prosperity in the farm sector, and the agitation of the farmer died down. One way to assess approximately what did happen to farm income is by taking a look at the value of farm land. Presumably, the value of land reflects the expected income that can be derived from that land; therefore, if land values were falling, this would provide evidence that farm income, too, was falling. Conversely, when land values are rising, the assumption is that farm income is rising too.[10] A study by John Bowman carefully examines land values in the Midwest during the period 1860–1900, and his results suggest that farm income was rising substantially in the 1860s; that it was falling in the 1870s and rising again in the 1880s; and that it was roughly constant in the 1890s.[11] Most interestingly,

---

[10] Actually, it is more complicated than this, since it is necessary to adjust for capital improvements and changes in the general price level and to apply an appropriate discount rate. Since "expectations" determine land values, it is assumed that these are derived from the past trend in land income.

[11] John Bowman, "Trends in Midwestern Farm Values, 1860–1914" (Ph.D. diss., Yale Univ., 1964).

perhaps, the analysis shows that there was tremendous county-by-county variation in the relative income of farmers and that any broad picture obscures the degree to which this variation etched widely different patterns of prosperity among various farm groups in sub-regions of the whole area. Bowman's conclusions are also supported by Bogue's study of the corn belt in Iowa and Illinois, for which he examines farm mortgage foreclosure rates during these decades. The foreclosure rates in general suggest that the decade of the 1870s was indeed a period of real distress, with foreclosure rates higher than in the 1860s, the 1880s, or the 1890s.[12] Although requiring substantially more research, this evidence does not fit the pattern of long-run continuous farm distress. Rather, it does suggest that there were periods of rising income interrupted by a very difficult decade of falling income in the 1870s. Farther west, in Kansas, Nebsaska, and elsewhere, the most difficult decade was surely the 1890s.

There is no doubt that after 1896 farm income rose strikingly. It was a period of rising prices generally, but the prices of farm goods rose more rapidly than other prices. How do we explain the apparently erratic behavior of farm income before 1896 and the era of relative prosperity after 1896? A tentative hypothesis suggests itself from the following facts and empirical data: (1) Throughout the whole period 1865–1914 the demand for agricultural goods was increasing very rapidly. (2) Up to 1896 the increased supply of agricultural output came both from putting additional land of top quality into production and from increasing productivity. (3) Between 1900 and 1910 the amount of new land put into farms increased less rapidly than in previous decades. In effect, the best land had already been taken up and put into production by that time, and the quality of the new land available was lower. Between 1900 and 1914 there was little or no increase in total factor productivity in agriculture. Table XI·1 and Fig. XI·2 illustrate these trends.

The tentative hypothesis is this: between 1870 and 1896, increased demand was met by surges of movement into new rich lands of constant fertility, resulting in low prices and productivity gains being passed on to consumers in the form of lower prices. As a result, the returns to farmers were generally low. After 1896, however, supply could be increased only by adding poorer land or by more intensively farming existing land. Either way would raise the real costs of addi-

---

[12] Allan G. Bogue, *From Prairie to Corn Belt* (Chicago: Univ. of Chicago, 1963), p. 179.

TABLE XI · 1 NEW LAND PUT INTO FARMS, 1870–1914	
Period ▼	Thousand Acres ▼
1860–70	61.6 ⎫
1870–80	134.9 ⎪
1880–90	187.1 ⎬ Yearly average
1890–1900	117.2 ⎪
1900–10	66.9 ⎭
1910–11	19.0
1911–12	5.0
1912–13	7.0
1913–14	10.0
1914–15	11.0

Source: *Hist. Statistics*, Ser. K 2, p. 278.

Fig. XI · 2   TOTAL FACTOR PRODUCTIVITY, 1869–1955

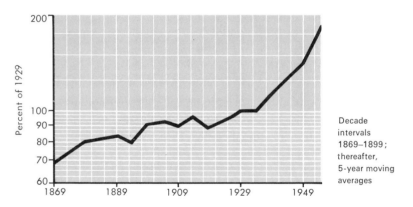

Decade intervals 1869–1899; thereafter, 5-year moving averages

Source: John W. Kendrick, *Productivity Trends in the United States* (Princeton, N.J.: Princeton Univ., 1961), pp. 362–64.

tional output, but it would also substantially increase returns for the best land in cultivation.

This explanation makes sense for agricultural commodities in the home market; nevertheless, it requires modification for commodities like wheat in the international market. If the hypothesis is universally valid, new lands put into production after 1900 in Canada, Australia, and elsewhere must have been less fertile than the best land put into production in the United States between 1865 and 1896.

CREATION OF AN
INDUSTRIAL GIANT AND
PROBLEMS OF MONOPOLY, 1860–1914

The Civil War was not a major impetus to accelerated industrial growth in America. This acceleration and the development of manufacturing had taken place before the war. But in the years from the end of the Civil War until World War I, manufacturing expanded so that the United States became the leading industrial nation in the world, with about one-third of the world's manufacturing capacity. The story of this industrial expansion is one of technological inventions fully exploited by entrepreneurs in an environment hospitable to such development. We can get a brief picture of this enormous expansion by looking at four cases that illustrate the combination of technological development with organizational ability responsible for this development.

Technology and organization: four industries

Steel certainly played a preeminent role. Iron had been the primary material used, along with wood, in machinery and in most durable goods. Then in the 1850s, Henry Bessemer developed a process that (along with a similar development by William Kelly in the United States) revolutionized the manufacture of steel. Superior to wrought iron, having much greater tensile strength and hardness, steel rapidly replaced iron in many uses (most important, in rails) as its price came down with the development of the Bessemer process. But quality control was difficult in the Bessemer process, and each batch of steel tended to vary. The open-hearth process, developed in the 1860s, was slower and initially more expensive; but because it enabled far better quality control and could make use of scrap, it gradually replaced the Bessemer process. Both methods originally could use only a narrow range of iron ores, excluding any with substantial amounts of phosphorus. The development of a basic lining that absorbed these impurities was a later important development, first used in an open-hearth furnace in 1880.

Both the Bessemer and the open-hearth processes are most efficient when they are used in large-scale production; consequently, the new industry gradually developed large firms. In 1872, Andrew Carnegie launched Carnegie Steel Limited to manufacture steel rails. As time went on, he and his partners absorbed other firms and plants. In those days, the large amount of coal required to make steel (two tons for every ton of iron ore) led to the location of mills adjacent to coal fields. Carnegie combined organizational ability with access to the capital market and acquired or built successive plants to meet the expanding requirements of the steel industry. Other firms also developed. Figure XII·1, p. 142, shows the rapid expansion of the steel industry as it rose from a mere 19,000 tons in 1867 to 10 million tons by 1900. As Andrew Carnegie is associated with the early developments of the steel industry, J. P. Morgan, financier, is associated with its giant consolidation and with the first billion-dollar corporation in the world. In 1901, Morgan pulled together all of Carnegie's properties, along with those of other major steel firms in the United States, to form the United States Steel Corporation.

The story of petroleum is somewhat different. There were no awaiting markets for the sticky substance that oozed out of the ground in western Pennsylvania. It was regarded as a nuisance. Initially, interest was attracted to it for its possible use as an ingredient in patent medicine, and a number of eastern interests sent a "Colonel" Drake out to see what could be done. It was Drake who conceived the idea of pumping the oil out of the ground. Once out and refined, the middle-weight distillates such as kerosene became the main lighting source in America until they were replaced later by gas and electricity. The refineries built in the 1860s were small, costing little more than $400; but by 1880 a refinery cost $300,000, and by 1900, $1.3 million. As in the steel industry, the development of large-scale production and improvements in methods lowered the cost; the price of petroleum fell from 36 cents a gallon in 1863 to 8 cents gallon in 1885.

Organization and development of the petroleum industry is inex-

Fig. XII · 1   STEEL OUTPUT (INGOTS, CASTINGS)

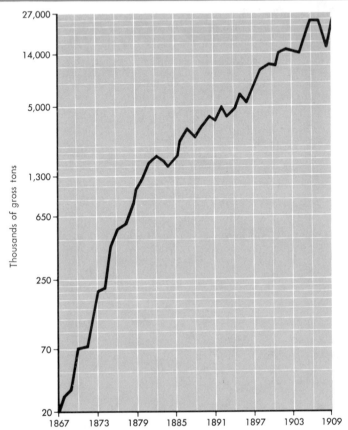

Source: Reprinted from *Iron and Steel in Nineteenth-Century America, An Economic Inquiry* by Peter Temin, by permission of the M.I.T. Press, Cambridge, Massachusetts. Copyright © 1964 by the Massachusetts Institute of Technology.

tricably associated with John D. Rockefeller. He consolidated the industry and initiated cheap transport methods, either by pressuring the railroads into developing them or by acquiring and developing pipelines for inexpensively carrying petroleum products to leading markets. Indeed, by the turn of the century, the Standard Oil Company came to dominate the refining part of the industry completely, just as a new demand for petroleum products was appearing with the use of the internal combustion engine in the new automobile.

The electrical industry, unlike steel, had its theoretical problems solved rather early—many of them by Michael Faraday. The industry was waiting chiefly for the development of a satisfactory dynamo; and in this invention, Thomas Edison played a leading role. Edison, virtually synonymous with the electrical industry, was an unusual combination in American history: he was an inventor, innovator, and often an entrepreneur. Like most entrepreneurs, however, even Edison made mistakes. A serious error was his persistence in using direct current even while other growing firms were stressing alternating current as a more advantageous means of distributing and using electricity. Nevertheless, Edison developed a host of uses for electricity, in which the electric light bulb and the whole system of electric lighting were critically important. The electricity industry became vital to manufacturing. The electric motor, especially designed for specific machines, made possible their more specialized and efficient use. Before Edison's time, an overhead belt (powered by a central source of steam or water power) had driven machines at a constant speed or at speeds varied by some system of reduction. An individual electric motor made it possible to turn off any machine or to operate each at a pace to match its particular function. Another development, the application of electricity to household appliances, continues even in the twentieth century as an industry of first-rate importance. Figure XII·2, p. 144, shows the value of electrical appliances produced from the end of the nineteenth century until 1938.

The automobile industry began at the end of the nineteenth century and has continued its major impact on the economy well into the twentieth century. For a long time, men had been experimenting with various devices for gaining locomotion by some automatic power. One of James Watts' partners experimented with a steam-powered automobile at a very early date; and in the 1860s and 1870s in France and Germany, numerous experiments were underway with various kinds of automobiles and with the internal combustion engine, which ultimately became the main source of power. There was a long period of experimentation and debate about what kind of engine and fuel would prove most efficient. Should it be electric or steam or internal combustion? Even after this question was settled—for the time being, anyway—there remained a period of adjustment in designing a body style that once and for all would dissociate the automobile from the carriage-without-a-horse concept.

Henry Ford took well established features of the internal combustion engine, and combined them with a design that was definitely an automobile, not a horseless carriage. Then, using the ideas first

Fig. XII · 2   VALUE OF HOUSEHOLD ELECTRICAL APPLIANCES PRODUCED, 1899–1938 (in millions of dollars)

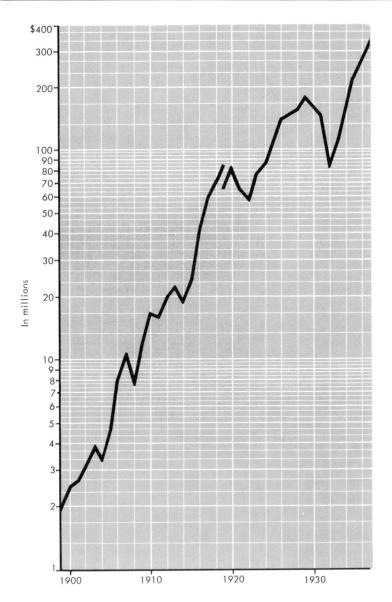

Source: *Hist. Statistics* (Washingotn, GPO, 1960), Ser. p. 250–306, p. 420.

developed by Eli Whitney regarding interchangeable parts and mass production, he formed an assembly line. The net result was a cheap, mass-produced Model T, foreshadowing today's traffic jams. Figure XII·3 illustrates the spectacular growth of the automobile industry from its early beginnings in 1899, when output was valued at only $4.2 million, until 1919, when it passed the billion-dollar mark.

Fig. XII · 3   OUTPUT OF PASSENGER MOTOR VEHICLES, 1899–1938

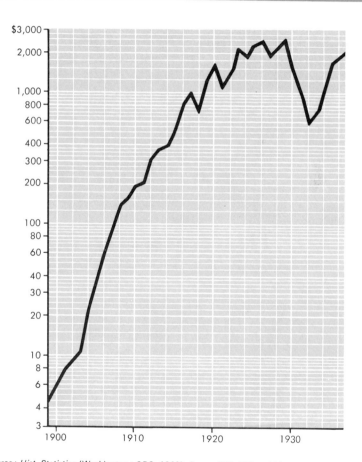

Source: *Hist. Statistics* (Washington: GPO, 1960), Ser. p. 250–306, p. 420.

These brief case studies are illustrative of the dynamic changes in technology and in organizations in American industry. The results can be seen on Fig. XII·4, which shows the value added by manufacturing, in constant prices. In the 60-year period 1839-1899, there is a fortyfold increase in this measure of manufacturing output.

The sources of expansion

What factors made possible this immense expansion? At the outset, it is necessary to separate two distinct aspects of this development: (1) the technological innovations that made possible the tremendous strides in industrial development, and (2) special factors that made American manufacturing development increase at a rate greater than that in the rest of the world.

The technological changes described above were but a small sample of revolutionary changes in almost every type of manufacturing. The origin of these innovations was not confined to the United States; in fact, many of them occurred in England, France, and Germany. Their development was accelerated by the rapid growth of scientific knowledge in the late nineteenth century and by the rising incomes and rapidly expanding demand that characterized the Western world. Despite the appearance of several interesting studies, the theory of technological change is still primitive.[1]

The relative increase in the United States' share of the world's goods reflected the combination of rapidly increasing population and growing productivity. It is easy at this point to become involved in circular reasoning over (1) whether manufacturing development was responsible for rising income or (2) whether the growing productivity of all resources was the source of expansion; and manufacturing growth, using new technology, was just one aspect of the development, given special impetus by the character of demand in this society (just as today's growing demand for services is leading to rapid expansion in that sector and relative decline in manufacturing). The second explanation is more consistent with the evidence of sources of productivity change. It is difficult to isolate particular attributes of manu-

---

[1] An important beginning has been made by Schmookler, Higgs, and Rosenberg. See the Bibliography for this chapter.

Fig. XII · 4 VALUE ADDED BY MANUFACTURING (1899 PRICES)

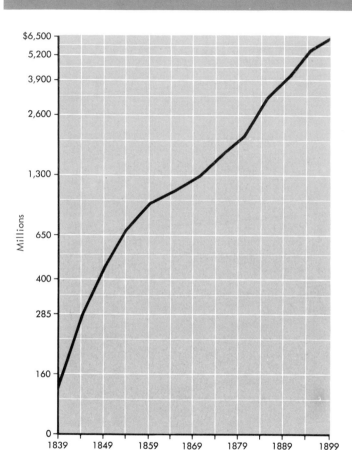

facturing productivity from the general increase in productivity that characterized American society during this period. One general source was the growing size of the American market. A large population having relatively high incomes made possible all potential economies of scale inherent in the technology of the individual industries.

An important initial influence was in the adaptation of foreign technology to fit American conditions (the relative prices of factors of production). The craftsmen, engineers, chemists, and other skilled members of the labor force were not just making use of existing equipment but were continually improvising and improving it as they went along, linking innumerable, sometimes indistinguishable separate innovations into technical advancement. This process reflected the quality of the labor force—the investment in human capital that distinguished the American work force—and the complementarity between human capital (engineers and scientists to make the essential modifications of technology) and physical capital (new or modified technology in the form of machinery, plant, and equipment).

American entrepreneurs are frequently singled out as the productive force that made possible the whole process. Their driving energy and often ruthless determination certainly led to new technology and its use in their large-scale organizations. Yet it is difficult to separate entrepreneurs from their environment and to credit the organizers with much responsibility for this expansion.[2] To the degree that certain entrepreneurial characteristics reflect the organizational skill learned on the job, credit goes to investment in human capital (in this case informal on-the-job training rather than formal education).[3]

Two other aspects of industrial growth should be mentioned. One has already been touched on—that America's labor supply was not purely indigenous, but augmented, especially in the last half of the nineteenth century, by sizeable immigration. More than a quarter of the population of Pennsylvania at the end of the nineteenth century was made up of immigrants, who formed a large part of the work force of the steel mills and coal mines. Later on, they became an important part of the automobile industry work force.

The other major factor is the development of the capital market; and this requires more discussion. In the first chapter, we said that capital broadly conceived has a more useful definition than the narrow, traditional meaning. Nevertheless, a further examination is needed of an efficient capital market, in the sense of organizing and channeling savings into the investments necessary to build factories and machinery, to clear and improve land, and to advance the working capital to maintain a labor force, inventories, and so forth.

While the focus here is upon the long-term capital market, it should be noted that in the years between the Civil War and World

---

[2] See R. P. Thomas, "The Automobile Industry and Its Tycoon, "*EEH*, VI (Winter 1969).

[3] The spread of formal education was important in the improving quality of the labor force. Since it has been the subject of examination in previous chapters, it needs no further emphasis here.

War I, the short-term market became more efficient.[4] The banking system expanded enormously in that period, both in the number of banks and in the amount of loans in circulation. It was not until the very end of the period that any semblance of central banking re-emerged in America—a reemergence from the long era of dispute following the end of the Second Bank of the United States, when Jackson vetoed its rechartering far back in the 1830s. With the Federal Reserve System, created in 1914, a central banking system was recon-structed, even though it was a decentralized one. However, the story of banking and the money supply properly belongs in a study of economic fluctuations and variations in the rate of utilization of re-sources—a subject to be explored in the next chapter.

The major concern here is with the evolution of the long-term capital market—that is, the evolution of a system of financial inter-mediaries that managed to get savings to flow into the industries that have been described in this chapter.[5] The growth of investment bank-ing in America traces its heritage back to the demand for large-scale financing for canals and railroads, to the development of a regular connection between English investors who wished to invest in Amer-ican railroads and American financial institutions. Gradually, some of the investment banks, having started as branches of English firms, developed into primarily American houses. They became organizers of large-scale financing of major industries. Savings were held in trust and savings banks, insurance companies, and other repositories, and the investment banker formed "syndicates" of financial groups to under-write the bond issues that went to build railroads, steel mills, agricul-tural machinery, factories, and other major projects. The growth of these savings institutions and financial intermediaries led to the in-creasing efficiency of the long-term capital market.

The heyday of monopoly

Investment banking inevitably conjures up the name of J. P. Morgan and Company, the famous investment banking firm that exercised enormous influence over the development of financial markets in

---

[4] "The Investment Market, 1870–1914," Lance Davis's previously cited article, provides evidence of the reduction of interregional short-term interest differentials and therefore the improvement in the short-term national capital market.

[5] Another facet of the long-term capital market was the farm mortgage market discussed in the previous chapter.

America. Morgan, more than anyone else, was responsible for railroad consolidation in the latter part of the nineteenth century; he also organized a number of the more celebrated mergers and consolidations at this time, the United States Steel Corporation being just one. If the investment banker performed the essential function of developing the long-term capital market and channeling the savings of Americans into industry, he also, by the end of the nineteenth century, posed a problem because of the growing consolidation of American business. This requires further examination.

As new industries developed in America and the pioneering firms earned large returns, these high returns attracted new firms into the industry. The resulting competition lowered prices and reduced the rates of return. It is not surprising that in the face of these reduced returns, businessmen attempted to collude. The entrepreneurs mentioned in the brief illustrations above were cited for their contributions to organization of the industry; some of them are equally celebrated for their role as ruthless promoters of collusive activities. Sometimes this collusion was nothing more than a pooling agreement that lasted only as long as the members kept a good eye on each other. Gradually, however, more sophisticated techniques were developed. In the 1880s, the trust became the typical form of enforcing agreements. The trust placed the control of a number of firms in the hands of a single board of directors; thus, no individual company could take advantage of price cutting to beat out its competitors, and all operated as a unit. The widespread creation of trusts caused such immense public reaction that in 1890 the Sherman Anti-Trust Act was passed, making trusts illegal and outlawing other monopolistic practices. It was many years later, however, before the Act became at all effective. The Northern Securities case of 1904, dissolving a famous railroad merger between E. H. Harriman and J. P. Morgan, and the even more spectacular dissolution of the Standard Oil Company in 1911 showed that the Sherman Act did have some teeth.[6]

The era around the turn of the century probably represented the high tide of mergers, and indeed of industrial concentration of major industries in the United States. Most observers believe that since that time, monopoly power—however defined—has not increased in America.

---

[6] A continuing problem for the courts was a good working definition of monopoly. Was it the percentage of the market that a firm controlled, the availability of close substitutes? Changing definition by the courts has led to changing policies.

What accounted for the upsurge of mergers during that period? It is easy to explain why mergers were regarded favorably by business, for their part in eliminating competition and raising returns, and why they frequently were initiated by the investment banker who received a handsome reward for forming the consolidation; it is somewhat more difficult to explain the lack of even further industrial concentration in subsequent years. Some observers have put stress upon the Sherman Antitrust Act, subsequent acts such as the Clayton Act, passed in 1914, and more vigorous prosecutions by the Antitrust Division of the Department of Justice. Others have pointed to the success of new entrants into the field, who have continuously overturned major firms; and the failure of large firms to hold their position in the economy in the face of competition from new firms suggests that this has, indeed, been important. Still others point to rapid technological change which continually creates new, superior products to compete successfully with older ones. Whatever the causes, it does appear that the period at the turn of the century was the heyday for monopoly power—at least to the extent that industrial concentration promotes such power.

WELFARE OF THE WORKER IN
THE ERA OF THE ROBBER BARONS

In this era of aggressive industrial expansion, of the development of giant industries, and of entrepreneurs who have been labeled robber barons, what happened to the worker? Whether he was the immigrant coming over from the Old World or the farm boy leaving the farm to seek his fortune in the city, he often found himself working in giant industrial firms and living in burgeoning cities filled with smoke, soot, filth, and conditions that, from our present perspective, hardly appear favorable.

Working conditions in the big manufacturing firms, as well as the social conditions of the sprawling new cities, certainly left much to be desired. Yet we must note carefully that the implicit hypothetical alternative suggested by such a comparison is with today's society, with today's productive capacity—many times that of the turn of the century. The relevant hypothetical alternative does not imply that the worker was exploited or that he experienced bad conditions by comparison with those of today; rather, it examines the extent to which the robber baron deprived the worker at that time. The lurid history of the aggressive entrepreneurs of the period leaves little doubt that they frequently robbed each other. How badly they victimized the worker, however, depended on the effectiveness of monopolies. The correct hypothetical alternative, therefore, is to examine what would have happened to per capita income in the absence of monopoly profits.

For society as a whole, monopoly is objectionable because restraints on free entry into any industry result in a misallocation of resources, so that total output in the economy is reduced.[7] Directly applicable to the issue we are exploring here, however, is (1) a measure of monopoly profits, and (2) the assumption that this was income that under competitive conditions would have gone to the rest of the population. By reassigning these profits to the rest of the population, we can see how much difference they would have made to per capita income. We note that in the years 1900 to 1909, corporate profits before taxes were 6.8 percent of the national income, which was approximately $20 billion at that time. This would make corporate profits about 1.4 billion.[8] If we take the figure $1.4 billion as profit and subtract from that the competitive rate of return on the nonfarm reproducible capital in America—that is, the rate that capital would have earned had all the corporate enterprises been competitive—then the residual will be a crude estimate of the "excess" profits of monopoly. We find that the reproducible tangible assets that are nonfarm are approximately $20 billion;[9] and if we assume 5 percent as a competitive rate of return, then $1 billion would be a competitive profit rate for all corporations. This leaves a monopoly residual of approximately $400 million. If we redistributed this amount among the total population of 1905, the resultant addition to per capita income would be slightly less than $5 each. Average per capita income was about $250

---

[7] Arnold Harberger attempts to measure the misallocation costs of monopoly for the late 1920s in "Monopoly and Resource Allocation," *AER*, XLIV (May 1954), 77–87. His conclusion is that they are small, but much controversy has been generated by his assumption of long-run constant costs.

[8] There were probably some "monopoly profits" in unincorporated income, although not enough to influence significantly the figures used here.

[9] The actual figure for corporate reproducible tangible assets is $25 billion ; however, I have allowed $5 billion for "watered" assets. This is certainly an overestimate of the extent to which this practice existed, but it serves to give an upward bias to the figure.

in current prices at that time, so that addition would represent a 2 percent increase in per capita income.

Although the above calculations suggest the income distribution effects of monopoly, a much more important issue is whether or not the worker was becoming better off at the turn of the century. A long-existing puzzle resulted from figures showing that not only in the United States, but in Britain and Germany as well, real wages of workers did not appear to rise very much between 1890 and 1914. The relevant study for the United States was one undertaken by Paul Douglas, which indicated that real wages showed no rise for the period as a whole. This seems paradoxical in the face of the enormous expansion of output, and it did suggest that in the U.S., as in Germany and Britain, monopoly must have adversely influenced workers' real wages. However, a new study by Albert Rees, *Real Wages in Manufacturing, 1890–1914,* under the auspices of the National Bureau of Economic Research, fundamentally revises this impression. Rees's figures show that hourly earnings adjusted by a new cost of living index rose significantly between 1890 and 1914, as Table XII·1 on p. 154 indicates. Indeed, new findings on Germany also suggest that the original impression of constant real wages in that country during the period needs revision as well.[10]

While these findings cast doubt that monopoly either pauperized the worker or prevented the growth of real wages, they in no way modify the long-standing view of the social historian that there were serious costs to society and to the worker in the crowded tenements, slums, and ghettos that grew up in major industrial cities during this period. In mid-nineteenth century America the death rate in large cities was approximately 30 per 1,000 while in the countryside it was around 20 per 1,000. Dense population accelerated the spread of communicable disease such as diphtheria and tuberculosis; poor diet also contributed. Water supplies and sewage disposal were often intermixed.

Beginning in the 1880s, substantial improvements were made, since they required the agreement of large numbers of people and the free rider problem was present, they could not usually be accomplished by voluntary organization, but required the powers of local governments. Health boards, compulsory vaccination against smallpox, tenement building codes, and public investment in water purification and

---

[10] V. Desai, *Real Wages in Germany, 1890–1914* (London : Oxford Univ., 1968).

sewage disposal yielded dramatic results. Water filtration alone reduced death rates dramatically.[11] The whole study of health in nineteenth-century America has been largely neglected and deserves much more attention in properly assessing our past economic experience.[12]

TABLE XII·1	**AVERAGE HOURLY EARNINGS, ALL MANUFACTURING, 1890–1914 (money and real terms)**		
	Average hourly earnings (current dollars) ▼	Cost-of-living index (1914 = 100) ▼	Average hourly earnings (1914 dollars) ▼
1890	0.144	91	0.158
1891	0.144	91	0.158
1892	0.145	91	0.160
1893	0.151	90	0.168
1894	0.139	86	0.162
1895	0.138	84	0.165
1896	0.144	84	0.172
1897	0.140	83	0.168
1898	0.137	83	0.166
1899	0.146	83	0.176
1900	0.151	84	0.179
1901	0.158	85	0.185
1902	0.165	86	0.191
1903	0.170	88	0.193
1904	0.169	89	0.190
1905	0.172	88	0.194
1906	0.184	90	0.204
1907	0.191	94	0.203
1908	0.184	92	0.201
1909	0.186	91	0.203
1910	0.198	95	0.209
1911	0.202	95	0.213
1912	0.207	97	0.213
1913	0.221	99	0.224
1914	0.220	100	0.220

Source: Albert Rees, *Real Wages in Manufacturing, 1890–1914* (Princeton: Princeton Univ., 1961), p. 4. Copyright 1961 by Princeton University Press.

[11] For a summary of the results, see Robert Higgs, *The Transformation of the American Economy, 1865–1914* (New York: Wiley, 1971), p. 70.

[12] A beginning has been made by Higgs, *ibid.*, pp. 36–39, 67–72, and by Ted Meeker, *The Economics of Improving Health, 1850–1915* (Ph.D. diss., Univ. of Washington, 1970). Meeker estimates that the social rate of return on improved sanitation and water supply was approximately 25 percent for a group of northeastern states during the period 1880–1910.

WAR, PROSPERITY, DEPRESSION, AND WAR, 1914–1945

Economic history of the twentieth century is a marked contrast to that of the nineteenth. The nineteenth century was one of growing international interdependence, unequaled movement of peoples from Europe to the newly settled lands of the rest of the world, and a flow of capital to aid in their development. The spread of new scientific ideas as embodied in technology led to growth in many parts of the world. In hindsight it is frequently argued that in the nineteenth century, development was limited to a small part of the world; however, in comparison to anything in the past, it was a century of unprecedented development, one in which man, by and large, could optimistically envision a continually expanding future. In contrast, the economic history of the twentieth century has been dominated by two global wars and a depression of unequaled severity—all leading to fundamental reorientation of the economy, to a new role for government, quite different from any it had occupied before, and to a far-from-optimistic view about the prospects of the world, in spite of the fact that the promise of modern technology is vastly greater than it was at the end of the nineteenth century.

Those roaring Twenties

War involved mobilization of resources and their diversion from the end objective of satisfying consumers in a peacetime economy to the immediate objective of effectively prosecuting a war. It is not surprising that when a war ends, the economy faces basic problems in dis-

155

location, in returning to the end objective of a consumer-oriented economy. During war, it is essential that a government control and direct the flow of resources for prosecuting the war; and when the war ends, the government tends not to release all of the controls. In 1919 with the end of World War I, however, the United States appeared well on its way back toward a consumer-oriented economy as demobilization took place on a substantial scale.

The first postwar cloud was the sharp, brief recession of 1921—a recession sometimes called an "inventory recession" because it has frequently been argued that it was caused by a rapid accumulation of inventories that could not then be sold at existing prices. The result was a sharp fall in prices and very brief unemployment distress, but thereafter the 1920s were a period of relative prosperity, marked by substantial growth, rising real wages of the worker, growing incomes, and particularly, expansion of the consumer durable goods industries. This was the decade in which the refrigerator, the radio, the gas or electric stove, and most notably the automobile became a part of most households in America. Mass production and low prices put automobiles and other consumer durable goods within the reach of most families.

Yet the decade was not prosperous for everyone. Even while incomes were steadily rising and the worker in manufacturing was increasing his standard of life, the farmer was struggling through a period of extremely low prices. We have already observed that the years from 1896 to 1914 were prosperous ones, followed by even more prosperous times during World War I, when the United States fed not only our own nation and army, but also our allies. The result was that agricultural prices rose sharply and farmers were encouraged to expand production immensely. When the war ended, the demand was substantially curtailed, as European countries erected tariff barriers to protect their own agriculture, and America in turn stopped the flow of immigration. Consequently, the demand for agricultural goods was substantially less than it had been earlier, and prices fell to extremely low levels.[1]

In the latter part of the decade, still another distressing sign appeared. This was the speculation in the stock market. From 1927 on,

---

[1] The demand for agricultural goods is income "inelastic"—that is, when incomes go up, people do not spend much more money on food. Therefore, an increasing demand for agricultural goods is primarily a result of more people. With immigration cut off, a major source of increased demand was eliminated.

and especially in 1929, the investors became convinced not only that prosperity was here to stay, but that they would make fortunes by buying stock and selling it at a tremendous profit after it had been bid up by everyone else. It appeared that everyone entered the stock market with this in mind; and as they did, they continued to bid up prices. Many speculators bought on margin, borrowing funds, so that with a very small amount of their own money they acquired large amounts of stock. This was workable as long as the stocks kept rising: they could pay off the mony they owed and still have substantial profits. But if the stock fell, that was something else again. The stock market disaster in the fall of 1929 was of an explosive character. There appeared to be no bottom. Stocks fell to such depths that they wiped out a tremendous number of investors, leaving them heavily indebted. Between 1929 and 1933, approximately four-fifths of the total value of stock disappeared. Table XIII·1 on p. 158 indicates what happened to the stock market in this period. The fall was so precipitous that it was not until the 1950s that stock prices recovered to their level of 1929.

The Great Depression examined

If the stock market was the trigger to this depression, it was certainly not the cause in a fundamental sense. The causes of depressions and cyclical instability are inherent in a free market economy. A market economy operates on the basis of the multiple decisions of consumers, savers, and investors. The producer plays a key role here, in that he must make decisions in advance with respect to buying his plant and equipment, buying raw materials, and employing workers, all before he receives any return. He is betting on what the demand will be for the goods he produces and, therefore, on what he will get in return. As a risk taker, he is willing to invest when expectations look bright. Conversely, if the economic barometer seems to be falling, he will batten down the hatches and curtail investment; and with the fluctuation in investment, income fluctuates: if businessmen do not invest, then income will fall, and this tends to have a cumulative impact. As less income becomes available, workers are laid off; when they are laid off and no longer able to buy more goods, the expectations of other businessmen who are investing look dimmer still, and they too curtail investments. This descending spiral keeps going.

The banking system can play, and indeed should play, an im-

TABLE XIII · 1   COLLAPSE OF STOCK MARKET

Year	Month, Day	Dow-Jones Industrial Averages High	Low
1925	November 6	159.39	
	October 14		99.18
1926	August 14	166.64	
	March 30		135.20
1927	October 3	199.78	
	January 25		152.73
1928	November 28	295.62	
	February 20		191.33
1929	September 3	381.17	
	November 13		198.69
1930	April 17	294.07	
	December 16		157.51
1931	February 24	194.36	
	December 17		73.79
1932	February 17	85.98	
	July 8		41.22
1933	July 18	108.67	
	February 27		50.16
1934	February 5	110.74	
	July 26		85.51
1935	November 19	148.44	
	March 14		96.71
1936	November 17	184.90	
	April 29		143.65
1937	March 10	194.40	
	November 24		113.64
1938	November 12	158.41	
	March 31		98.95
1939	September 12	155.92	
	April 8		121.44
1940	January 3	152.80	
	June 10		111.84

Source: Robert Rhea, *Graphic Charts: Dow-Jones Daily Stock Averages and Sales.* Privately published by permission of Dow Jones & Company, Inc., 1931.

portant role at this point. The ideal objective of monetary authorities, through their control and operation of the banking system, is to insure that in periods of declining expectations, the stock of money will expand and the cost of investing fall. That is, the objective of the banking authorities should be to attract investors at such periods; just as in periods of substantial inflation, the objective of the banking authorities is to discourage substantial expansion in the money supply and investing, in order to prevent rapid rises in prices when employment is full. The period from 1929 to 1932 is one which the role of the Board of Governors of the Federal Reserve and their member banks has been severely criticized, because it does not appear today that the Federal Reserve did anything about the spiraling depression. Their defenders have argued that in fact there was nothing that they could do, whereas the critics have maintained that the Federal Reserve never tried to do anything, although it had the power to increase member banks' reserves, thus expanding the money supply. Some critics have maintained that such a policy could have ended the Depression then and there. Whether or not this is true, it still is clear that the Federal Reserve was by and large passive during this period; and if anything, in September 1931 it further exacerbated the decline by raising the rediscount rate in order to prevent a gold drain.

The magnitude of the Depression can be judged from Fig. XIII·1 on p. 160, which shows the percentage of the labor force unemployed and Fig. XIII·2, p. 161, which shows the fall in per capita and total incomes. A quarter of America's labor force was unemployed in 1932 and 1933. There was no precedent for such tremendous unemployment in American history. Moreover, they remained unemployed; and although gradual recovery was taking place, a very substantial share of the labor force continued out of work during the whole decade. It is not surprising in the light of the anomalous character of the Depression that the government should be confused about what to do.

Under President Hoover, a first effort was made toward recovery by setting up the Reconstruction Finance Corporation, to make loans that would encourage business expansion in spite of bad times. With $1.5 billion available, the RFC was a step in the right direction, but the amount was too limited to block the swelling tide. A second effort was the Hawley-Smoot tariff act, raising tariffs but providing only some brief protection for some industries (in import-competing goods) at the expense of those engaged in exports. In order to help the farmer, Hoover set up the Farm Board. Its objective was to stabilize farm prices, but the $500 million appropriated for this purpose was soon exhausted, and thereafter prices continued to tumble.

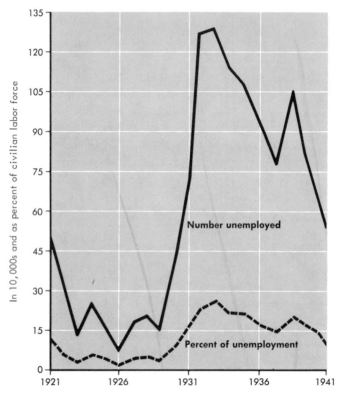

Fig. XIII·1   UNEMPLOYMENT, 1921–1941

Source: *Hist. Statistics* (Washington: GPO, 1960), Ser. D 46–47, p. 73.

The New Deal

When Franklin D. Roosevelt came into office in 1933, the depth of the Depression had been reached, and he faced a new dilemma in closing the banking system throughout the country. His first hundred days were marked by an unprecedented series of legislative acts designed to get the country back on its feet, and his success with the banking system was one that inspired confidence in many people. Banks were audited, and those that appeared to be fundamentally sound were reopened with encouragement and support from the government.[2]

---

[2] After a four-day banking holiday, an emergency banking act was passed, giving the RFC authority to support sound banks; and when banks judged to be sound were reopened, the fears of depositors were allayed.

His other legislation covered the whole gamut of activities of the New Deal, from setting up the Tennessee Valley Authority through the beginnings of the legislation toward social security. Let us first look at attempts to get out of the Depression, and then look at the other New Deal objective—reform.

Roosevelt's first effort to get out of the Depression was aimed at raising prices. The gold standard was abandoned, and gold was revalued, to encourage inflation. Next was the passage of the National Industrial Recovery Act. It permitted industries to collude and cartelize in order to raise prices and thereby give businessmen an incentive to produce. The Agricultural Adjustment Act (the heir of the old Farm Board) was designed to pay farmers to limit their production. It is easy in hindsight to see that these programs would not work. It would be hard to imagine that prices could be increased substantially in a period of such tremendous unemployment of resources or that industry collusion would encourage consumer demand. Nevertheless, they were groping and courageous efforts to stimulate the desperately ailing economy. The next efforts of the Roosevelt administration were aimed

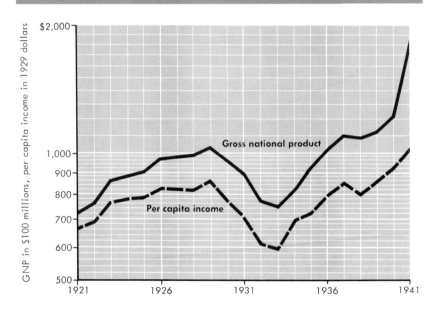

Fig. XIII · 2 NATIONAL PRODUCT AND INCOME, 1921–1941
(GNP in $100 millions, per capita income in 1929 dollars)

Source: *Hist. Statistics* (Washington: GPO, 1960), Ser. F 1–5, p. 139.

at what was called "priming the pump." In modern terms this is called deficit financing; it is a system whereby the government spends more than it takes in tax receipts. Obviously, deficit spending on its own would tend to encourage expansion, unless it led to curtailment of investment on the part of the private sector. Indeed, while Roosevelt was pragmatically experimenting with such activities, John Maynard Keynes was providing a theoretical justification for them in a revolutionary book in economics that advocated government deficit financing.[3] The problem with Roosevelt's "priming the pump" was that it was not enough and that the amount of deficit spending was so small that it was unable to lift the economy out of the depths to which it had fallen.

While the fundamental objective of the Roosevelt administration was recovery, a secondary one with lasting consequences was reform. A basic assumption underlying the operation of a market economy, badly shaken in a depression, is that it operates in a way that provides maximum welfare for its citizens, and that no tinkering by government can improve upon this set of conditions. Under the Roosevelt administration, this argument was swept aside in favor of one that maintained that governmental action could substantially improve the welfare of members of the society. Perhaps the most far-reaching of the legislation dealt with security for individuals. The security that once had depended upon close family unity was gradually disappearing in the face of the impersonal characteristics of an evolving market economy. The aged and the sick could no longer depend upon the family for security. Young people tended to underestimate what their needs would be in old age. A primary objective of a social security program was therefore to make provision for old-age security from the beginning of employment. With this objective in mind, Congress passed laws on old-age insurance, unemployment insurance, and workmen's compensation—all aimed at providing security for individuals under various kinds of duress and over different periods of their life.

A second area of reform was in securities and banking. The stock market crash as well as the failure of banks had convinced many that the underpinnings for each were faulty. The Banking Act of 1933 divorced investment banking from commercial banking, and the Securities and Exchange Commission was established to regulate the stock

[3] *The General Theory of Employment, Interest and Money* (New York: Harcourt, 1936).

market. The Federal Deposit Insurance Corporation was set up to insure fully bank deposits up to $10,000 (and a percentage above that figure), and the Banking Act of 1935 was passed to expand the authority of the Federal Reserve Bank in monetary affairs.

While the federal government expanded the powers and increased the number of regulatory agencies trying to improve the performance of business, the Norris-La Guardia Act (actually passed in 1932 prior to the New Deal) freed trade unions from the threat of injunction, and they were granted the right of collective bargaining first by section 7a of the National Industrial Recovery Act and subsequently as that provision was restated in the National Labor Relations Act of 1935.

A final area of government intervention was public investment in a variety of projects, of which the most noteworthy related to water resources. The Tennessee Valley Authority was established to develop an integrated multipurpose complex of dams for navigation, flood control, power, and recreation. In the Northwest, the Grand Coulee Dam provided power, but its ultimate objective was to irrigate a million acres of the Columbia Basin. The underlying assumption was that the gains to society from such activities—that is, social benefits—were greater than the private benefits and therefore were worthy undertakings, even if not privately profitable.

It is clear that by the end of the 1930s the role of government in the economy had changed fundamentally. It had increased as a result of efforts to get the economy out of the Depression, and it had increased on the assumption that the welfare of the society could be improved by government intervention to reorganize and reallocate resources in particular areas, in contrast to the way in which the markets would have allocated them.

How successful was the New Deal in its efforts? Its success with respect to recovery was certainly far from complete. By 1940, as the preceding charts show, 8 million people (almost 15 percent of the labor force) were still unemployed; 10 percent were still unemployed in 1941, when the economy had begun to gird for war. The recovery that had shown promise in 1935 and 1936 was set back severely in 1937. Again, the policies of the Board of Governors of the Federal Reserve have frequently been blamed, in that they raised reserve requirements in the beginning of that year, so that the economy again fell back into the depths, reemerging only by 1939. Certainly, the New

Deal did not cause complete recovery, but an evaluation of its degree of success would have to be made against some hypothetical, alternative set of policies. One thing is clear, however: what the New Deal failed to do, World War II did with vigor. Between 1941 and 1942, when we suddenly became involved in global war, we again became a full-employment economy, remarkably illustrating how we could expand output and productive capacity and reorient ourselves to prosecute a war in a fashion and to a degree that amazed our allies and dismayed our enemies.

WAS THE NEW DEAL A SOCIAL REVOLUTION?

The New Deal provided hope and encouragement to millions in a desperate era; it also produced violent epithets from businessmen and conservatives generally. Yet, viewed from a more detached perspective of more than a generation, what were the long-run consequences of the New Deal in terms of its effect on the welfare of American society? Was the New Deal really a new deal? Presumably, if it was, it (1) brought about a more fully employed economy, (2) accelerated the rate of growth of the economy, or (3) redistributed income in favor of that one-third of the nation who were ill-clothed, ill-housed, and ill-fed, to use Franklin D. Roosevelt's famous phrase. In order to do a careful appraisal, it would be necessary to spell out what hypothetical alternative we had in mind in each case. However, the necessary research has not yet been done, and at this point all we can do is to provide a more limited appraisal of the influence of New Deal policies.

With respect to full employment, we have observed that during the 1930s the New Deal failed to accomplish its objective. Failure is not surprising in the light of governmental fiscal policy. A careful examination yields the conclusion.[4] (1) In only two years during the 1930s was governmental fiscal policy (at all levels) significantly more expansionary (in terms of its effect on aggregate demand) than it had been in 1929. The two exceptions were 1931 and 1936, when large payments to veterans were made over the objection of both the Hoover and the Roosevelt administrations. (2) Federal government fiscal

---

[4] E. C. Brown, "Fiscal Policy in the 'Thirties : A Reappraisal," *AER*, XLVI, No. 6 (Dec. 1956).

policies were somewhat more expansionary (in part as a result of the veterans' payments, opposed by the executive branch) than were state and local government policies; and when all three are taken together, they about cancel each other out in terms of any significant net effect. (3) The primary reason for this ineffectiveness was that tax rates at every level of government expanded. All governments combined had run a deficit (spent more than they collected in taxes) in 1929, but from 1933 to 1939 (except 1936) all governments either ran a surplus (took in more than they spent) or had an approximately balanced budget.

Yet, the New Deal left one heritage that appears to have played an influential part in maintaining high levels of employment and income in periods of subsequent recession. These are the social security measures of old-age and survivors' unemployment insurance, and workmen's compensation. In periods of recession, they have maintained the income of unemployed workers and tended to limit the fall in income and to prevent the vicious spiral results described earlier. Social security measures appear to have developed some important, built-in stabilizers for mitigating subsequent recessions.

Did the New Deal affect the overall growth rate of the economy? There is certainly no clear evidence on this subject. One would except that New Deal measures that might have had some effect were (1) setting up regulatory bodies designed to improve the performance of business, with the result, presumably, of improving resource allocation, and (2) undertaking projects in areas where public investment might be assumed to have a higher social rate of return than private rate of return. Certainly, however, the results in both cases are equivocal at best. The regulatory bodies at times may have accomplished some improvements in resource allocation and industry performance; at other times, they proved to be handmaidens to the industries themselves, making unwise resource allocation and hampering rather than benefiting the performance of the industry. A continuing dilemma of regulatory agencies is that they can become vehicles whereby the regulated regulate the regulators, in the interest of the regulated—rather than that of the public.

I know of no overall appraisal of government investment in water resources during the New Deal period. Perhaps the most important contribution was the impetus it gave to developing benefit–cost analysis, so that we could measure the rate of return on such projects and eventually extend our analysis to other types of government activity.

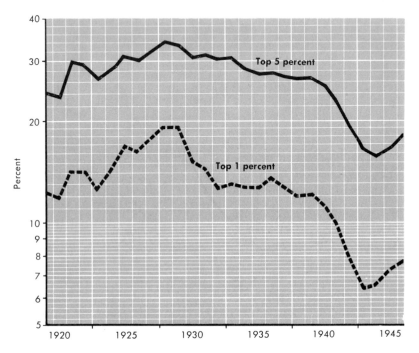

Fig. XIII · 3   PERCENT OF DISPOSABLE INCOME RECEIVED BY TOP INCOME GROUPS (total population, 1919–1946)

Source: *Hist. Statistics* (Washington: GPO, 1960), Ser. G 131–46, p. 167.

In many respects, the third issue was the one around which New Deal policy at the time became most controversial: the redistribution of income in the United States. For if the New Deal did not achieve full employment and if its implications for growth are at best equivocal, then the only way it could have benefited that one-third of the nation was by redistributing income in its favor, and clearly the New Deal intended such results in a number of its policies. Specifically, policies that were aimed at encouraging the growth of trade unions—such as the National Labor Relations Act and the Norris–LaGuardia Act—had the objective of expanding unionism in America, and it was commonly assumed that unions would thereby increase income going to labor. These acts, together with the rivalry that developed between the American Federation of Labor and the newly created Congress of Industrial Organizations, did expand trade union membership from about 3 million in 1932 to 9 million in 1940. Similarly, the Fair Labor

Standards Act, establishing minimum wages for workers, aimed at benefiting the lowest-income groups. The price-support program in agriculture, the subsidized low-cost housing for low-income groups, and the social security program were all aimed in this direction. What were their results?

Figure XIII·3 shows disposable income of the 1 percent and top 5 percent of income groups between 1919 and 1946, and Fig. XIII·4 shows the share of the top 1 per cent of wealth-holders in the United States. Both charts show that wealth and income were becoming more unequally distributed in the 1920s, and both show a fall, after 1929, in the percentage of wealth and income of the top holders. In the period from 1933 to 1939, wealth-holding again became somewhat more unequal, but the share of the top income-holder continued to fall throughout. The significant decline in inequality comes in the war years, however. It is equally evident that after the war, wealth and income again became somewhat more unequally distributed. During the Thirties, there was a decline in the share of the highest-income groups, but it appears to have gone to middle-income groups. The lowest 20 percent of consumer units, in terms of their income, received 4.1 percent of total family personal income in 1935; they received 5 percent in 1947 and 4.6 percent in 1962.

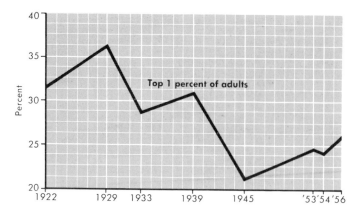

Fig. XIII·4 **SHARE OF PERSONAL SECTOR WEALTH HELD BY TOP WEALTH-HOLDERS, SELECTED YEARS, 1922–1956**

Source: Robert J. Lampman, *Tha Share of Top Weath-Holders in National Wealth, 1922–56*, A Study by the NBER (Princeton N.J.: Princeton Univ., 1962), p. 25. Copyright 1962 by Princeton Univ. Press.

In summary, it is not at all clear that New Deal measures provided any significant redistribution of income. The fall in the share of top wealth- and income-holders came about as a result of the Depression in 1929, so there had been a significant decline by the time the New Deal started. The really significant fall is clearly related to the high progressive tax rates imposed during World War II. Moreover, the redistribution from the very rich appears to favor middle-income rather than lowest-income groups.

A careful examination of the measures designed to effect this income redistribution suggests that this overall result is not surprising. If incomes were being redistributed in the 1930s, it was because the laws that were passed either facilitated a relative rise in the low-income group or transferred income from high-income groups to low-income groups. Minimum wage laws and promotion of trade unions were aimed at facilitating a relative rise in the low-income group, but their effectiveness in redistributing income in favor of low-income groups is debatable. It is not at all self-evident that minimum wage laws really raised wages of low-income groups. To the extent that they are effective, and that the minimum wage exceeds that value of output of workers, the long-run result will be more unemployment and therefore more inequality in income. Similarly, even though trade unions may raise wages of their members, it is a much debated point whether they raised wages over all. Labor's share of national income appears to have been increasing, but this is certainly not attributable to trade unions.[5] Therefore, if trade unions do manage to raise their wages but do not influence labor's share of national income, then they do so at the expense of three-quarters of the labor force, which is unorganized.[6] Since this includes most of the lowest-wage earners, the result appears likely to have made incomes more unequal, rather than more equal.

More effective results surely stem from the direct transfers of

---

[5] Labor's share of national income appears to have been increasing since about 1910, long before trade unions had any appreciable effect on the economy. A partial explanation is in the shift out of agriculture (self-employed entrepreneurial income) into wage status; but this is not a complete explanation. See Irving B. Kravis, "Relative Income Shares in Fact and Theory," *AER*, XLIX, No. 5 (Dec. 1959), 917–49.

[6] The impact of trade unions upon wages has been the subject of extensive inquiry. A recent study by H. G. Lewis (*Unionism and Relative Wages in the United States: An Empirical Enquiry*. Chicago: Chicago Univ., 1963) summarizes previous studies along with the author's own investigations. The result is an indispensable study for those who wish enlightenment on this controversial issue.

income from high- to low-income groups, as in the case of public housing and welfare payments. Their magnitude in the Thirties does not appear to have been significant, although the slight increase in the position of the lowest quintan of income earners in the 1940s suggests that the highly progressive tax rates combined with welfare measures in that decade temporarily improved the status of the lowest-income group. But that modest result came after the New Deal.

THE MODERN DILEMMA:
GOVERNMENT AND THE ECONOMY

Today's economy is fundamentally different from the economy of previous centuries. The market place has seen a basic change in the mix of economic activity undertaken by government and by voluntary organizations. The size, composition, and level of each sector have also changed: the size of government has increased immensely, at the expense of voluntary organizations and the market; the composition and level of government activities have been sharply transformed.

Government's new role

Tables XIV·1 and XIV·2, pp. 171, 172, are a striking picture, even though the figures are in current, inflated dollars, which somewhat exaggerate the growth in expenditure. The really startling expansion of federal government expenditure has occurred since the beginning of World War II. Although conservative opinion in the 1930s held that the Roosevelt administration was spending us into bankruptcy, in retrospect the growth of federal expenditure appears quite modest. The major change in the 1930s was the growth of regulation of business, a subject to which we shall return. The great expansion of local and state government occurred in the post-World War II era, and today state and local expenditures are increasing at a more rapid rate than federal expenditures.

The sources of the growth are readily observable in Table XIV·2. Military expenditures account for almost half of federal government expenditures. In recent years expenditures aimed at improving the lot of the poor—such as the farm subsidy program and some of the pro-

TABLE XIV·1	EXPENDITURES OF THE FEDERAL, STATE, AND LOCAL GOVERNMENTS (in billions)	
Calender Year ▼	Federal Government ▼	State and Local Government ▼
1929	$ 2.6	$ 7.8
1930	2.8	8.4
1931	4.2	8.5
1932	3.2	7.6
1933	4.0	7.2
1934	6.4	8.1
1935	6.5	8.4
1936	8.7	9.0
1937	7.4	8.6
1938	8.6	8.1
1939	8.9	9.6
1940	10.0	9.3
1941	20.5	9.1
1942	56.1	8.8
1943	85.1	8.4
1944	95.5	8.5
1945	84.6	9.0
1946	35.6	11.0
1947	29.8	14.3
1948	34.9	17.4
1949	41.3	20.0
1950	40.8	22.3
1951	57.8	23.7
1952	71.0	25.3
1953	77.0	27.0
1954	69.7	29.9
1955	68.1	32.7
1956	71.9	35.6
1957	79.6	39.5
1958	88.9	44.0
1959	91.0	46.8
1960	93.0	49.6
1961	102.1	54.1
1962	110.3	57.6
1963	113.9	62.2
1964	118.1	67.8
1965	123.5	74.5
1966	142.8	83.9
1967	163.6	95.1
1968	181.5	107.5
1969	189.5	118.9
1970	205.1	132.9

Source: *Economic Report of the President*, transmitted to Congress January 1972. Table B-70, p. 277.

TABLE XIV · 2	FEDERAL, STATE, AND LOCAL GOVERNMENT EXPENDITURE, BY FUNCTION, 1902–1970 (in millions of dollars)

Year ▼	Total expen-diture ▼	Nat'l. defense ▼	Edu-cation ▼	High-ways ▼	Public welfare ▼	Govt. payments to farm landlords ▼	HEM ▼	HUD ▼
1902	1,660	165	258	175	41			
1913	3,215	250	582	419	57			
1922	9,297	875	1,713	1,296	128			
1927	11,220	616	2,243	1,819	161			
1932	12,437	721	2,325	1,766	445	10		
1934	12,807	553	2,005	1,829	979	–		
1936	16,758	932	2,365	1,945	997	50		
1938	17,675	1,041	2,653	2,150	1,233	–		
1940	20,417	1,590	2,827	2,177	1,314	60		
1942	45,576	26,555	2,696	1,765	1,285	–		
1944	109,947	85,503	2,805	1,215	1,150	–		
1946	79,707	50,461	3,711	1,680	1,435	70		
1948	55,081	16,075	7,721	3,071	2,144	–		
1950	70,334	18,355	9,647	3,872	2,964	20		
1952	99,847	48,187	9,598	4,714	2,830	–		
1953	110,054	53,583	10,117	5,053	2,956	–		
1954	111,332	49,265	11,196	5,586	3,103	–		
1955	110,717	43,472	12,710	6,520	3,210	20		
1956	115,796	42,680	14,161	7,035	3,185	–		
1957	125,463	45,803	15,098	7,931	3,453	–		
1958	134,931	46,127	16,836	8,702	3,866	–		
1959	145,748	48,389	18,119	9,726	4,193	–		
1960	151,288	47,464	19,404	9,565	4,462	60		
1961	164,875	49,387	21,214	9,995	4,779	–		
1962	176,240	53,225	22,814	10,508	5,147	–		
1963	184,027	54,102	24,869	11,253	5,572	–	–	–
1964	196,231	54,899	27,509	11,972	6,132	190	–	–
1965	205,550	55,810	29,613	12,348	6,420	220	–	–
1966	212,340	70,881	35,313	13,341	7,919	300	–	–
1967	257,800	74,638	40,214	14,032	9,592	280	35,133	2,793
1968	282,645	83,874	43,614	14,654	11,245	310	40,576	4,140
1969	308,344	84,496	50,377	15,738	14,730	340	46,259	2,017
1970	332,985	84,253	55,771	16,746	17,517	330	52,249	2,603

Sources: For 1902–1957, *Hist. Statistics*, Ser. Y 412–45, p. 723. For 1958–1962, *Continuation of Hist. Statistics*, 1965, p. 99. U.S. Bureau of the Census, *Statistical Abstract of the United States: 1972*, pp. 410, 596.

grams of Health, Education and Welfare—have been increasing. At the state and local level, much of the growth is due to highways, education, and welfare.

Sources of government expansion

It is easy enough to discover the sources of the expansion; it is much more controversial to assess the consequences. Let's take them in turn. The initial impetus for increasing military expenditures has come from global war on an unprecedented scale and the tremendous costs of new military technology. The growth of educational expenditure mirrors the view (discussed in Chapter VIII) that the return to society is higher than the return to the individual and that education should not be denied those who cannot pay. The postwar impetus has been further spurred by research that points to investment in human capital as a major contributor to economic growth. The spectacular growth in higher education emanates from a conviction that the investment in going beyond high school is increasingly worthwhile. With so many on their side, schools have been getting increasing per capita help from the states and unprecedented expansion in federal aid to public higher education.

Between 1940 and 1970 the number of automobiles increased from 22 million to 106 million; now more than one for every two people in the country. Trucks have progressively displaced railroads in hauling goods. The growth in road and highway expenditure is an inevitable consequence.

Ever since the era of the New Deal there has been a persistent and growing conviction that poverty in the richest country in the world is an anomaly. This conviction has spawned a vast array of programs at the federal and state level. The farm price support program, the Office of Economic Opportunity, and myriad state welfare programs all have one ostensible purpose in common: to redistribute income from the more affluent to the poor.

The consequences of government

When we turn to examine the consequences, some are readily predictable from our analysis of nonmarket decision making (Chapter II). The government purchases its military equipment from a number of firms that specialize in producing such equipment. These firms have only one purchaser, and their stake in receiving orders is their very survival. It is not surprising therefore that they have intimate and powerful political ties with the federal bureaucracy and officeholders. The "military-industrial complex" is not an aberration but the logical consequence of voluntary organizations whose welfare or survival depends on federal government spending. Nor is it unique; it has its counterpart in every other voluntary organization that depends on government spending at every level. Teacher organizations are among the most powerful state lobbies, although hardly more powerful than contractors and the construction unions that build highways; even welfare recipients have become a powerful political force.

As we noted above, these are the obvious and immediate consequences. Some of the other consequences are the major issues of our times. Quite aside from actual war itself, the potential destruction in the store of military weapons is staggering to contemplate. It is no longer self-evident that the educational system is an unmitigated good or even that there is a very high rate of return on higher education. Not only are we less sure that we are producing the right amount of education; we do not even have a clear idea of what it is we are trying to produce. That is, we do not have a good measure of "output." We have built highways until they threaten to pave over the nation, and we drive automobiles that are the prime source of pollution in America, pouring forth 230,000 tons of carbon monoxide into our air each day. Finally, despite approximately $30 billion expended annually on the poor, there is no conclusive evidence that the share of income going to the lowest income receivers has risen very much. What's the matter?

It is easier to understand the problems than to solve them. A careful reading of Chapter II makes clear that the consequences of making economic decisions via the market place will be very different from making them via the political process. Take education for example. The "ideal" amount from the standpoint of efficiency would be where an additional dollar spent on education yielded a social rate of return just equal to that of a dollar spent anywhere else in the society. That assumes that we could measure educational output properly, so we could compare it to other investment returns. But even if we could, the various interest groups being subsidized—middle-income parents, teachers, and the students themselves—have a direct political stake that gives them more clout than the general electorate, and they fare correspondingly better.

Or take the automobile. The polluter is the driver—that is, the general public—and the public has shown no inclination to tax itself so that private and social costs would be equated. What politician would survive in Los Angeles (where 90 percent of the smog is from automobile exhaust) if he argued for a $5.00 toll charge on every car coming onto the freeways that interlace the city? And mass transit is not an acceptable substitute to the average driver until he is forced to it by much higher charges (i.e., making private costs approach social costs) on the highways.

When we look at the poverty program, the explanation is simple: most of the funds never get to the poor; they feed a vast and growing bureaucracy at federal and state levels, or they go to other recipients (such as large-scale farmers in the case of the farm price support program).

Do we fare better when we regulate the private sector rather than involving government directly in production? From the inception of the Interstate Commerce Commission in 1887, the market place has increasingly been limited by regulatory bodies. They proliferated with the "alphabet soup" of the New Deal (AAA, SEC, NRA, CAB, and others) and have continued to expand both at federal and state levels ever since. The ICC, founded to regulate the railroad in the public interest, was created despite considerable opposition from some of the railroads, yet the railroads immediately found that they could accomplish with the ICC what they had failed to accomplish in the market place; that is, they now had an effective vehicle of cartelization to set and enforce prices. Many regulatory agencies have had a similar fate: they have (predictably) been taken over by the very groups they are supposed to regulate; and equally predictably, the bureaucracy continues to expand in each case. In some cases—particularly in eras of reform or new politics—the regulatory body, in its zeal, sets prices so low that it is unprofitable to expand production, and we have shortages (e.g., in natural gas and electric power).

Before you conclude that the world must have been fine before government got into the act, remember those noisome, polluted nineteenth-century towns and cities with their open sewers and coal smog, the illiteracy of the eighteenth century, and the lack of protection by law and the Constitution. In fact, it's easy to define the dilemma. Where there are substantial differences between private and social benefits and costs, then we would like to narrow the gap if it can be done economically. Sometimes it can be done by a better or more complete specification of private property rights, but often problems of measurement of benefits and costs (and behind them, as we have seen, even output itself) make this solution unfeasible (at least with present technology). We can bring the dilemma into sharp focus by examining a classic issue that has long historical antecedents.

GROWTH VERSUS THE ENVIRONMENT

Ever since man came out of the trees he has been destroying the environment. Even with primitive weapons he brought destruction (and extinction) to many wild animals. As settlement replaced hunting he girdled the trees, destroyed forests, and burned over the land. When he huddled together in settlements he produced pollution of air and water. So what's new? There's nothing new except the magnitude of the issue and the means of solution at hand.

Whenever something became scarce, man had an incentive to develop property rights over it because its potential value had risen. We have seen in Chapter II that if this could be done cheaply (if the benefits exceeded the costs), then he had an incentive to husband and improve the resource, since private property rights allowed the individual owner to capture more of the gains.

The illustrations mentioned above were not a major concern as long as there appeared to be endless forests and unlimited amounts of clean air and clean water, but by the end of the nineteenth century these conditions no longer held. We have already discussed the polluted mill towns of the new industrial society. The cut-over forests of New England and the upper Midwest were already shifting timber companies to the Pacific Northwest and the South when Gifford Pinchot and Theodore Roosevelt were expressing concern for the condition of the natural environment.

What is different today is the magnitude of the problem. Two hundred million people living in the close proximity of an urban world continually affect each other so that externalities—third party effects— are a ubiquitous characteristic of our society. There is literally a mountain of waste material to be disposed of each day; we have already mentioned the volume of carbon monoxide from the automobile; we need power, but dams inundate scarce wilderness areas; coal-fired generating plants pollute the air, and nuclear plants heat the water and (at least potentially) emit radiation.

One solution is simply to build no more power plants, and indeed today environmentalists, via the courts and class action suits, are halting construction of new power facilities on a massive scale. The consequences now—and even more in the future—are brownouts, blackouts, and higher power rates. Moreover, to the extent that the poor pay a larger share of their income than the rich pay for power, the rise in rates hits them the hardest.

A continuous search for new technologies without deleterious side effects is in progress, but we cannot, at least in the short run, feel confident of great results.

A third alternative, to bridge the interim until such new techniques are developed, is to measure the actual social costs and benefits of alternative means of developing power, so that we can actually know who gets hurt and by how much and who benefits and by how much

Benefit—cost analysis attempts to do just that. It is difficult but not impossible to measure the benefits of a wilderness area or of preserving a salmon run, as well as to measure the costs of air pollution. It is also possible, within limits, to discover who benefits and by how much and who bears the costs. In short, we must measure the side effects. Then we are at least in position to charge individuals and firms for the social costs of their behavior (rather than just the private costs), which provides them with the incentive to reduce pollution. The result is surely a lower rate of observed growth (although not necessarily actual growth, since if we measured output properly it would take into account social costs and benefits), but this strategy offers the promise of enabling man to live with his environment.

However, it is one thing to measure the side effects; it is something else actually to impose the social costs. In earlier parts of this chapter we observed that the political ramifications of imposing the true social costs on "polluters" made this an unlikely solution, and the reasoning in Chapter II provides an explanation of why this is so. We must improve our understanding of how a political economy operates, so that we can devise effective political solutions. This is a challenge as old as the controversies that swirled around the framers of the Constitution, but it now possesses a new urgency. The economic means are at hand to get better measures of social costs and benefits and therefore to improve social economic performance. The question remains: can we make government responsive so that it can implement these means?

BIBLIOGRAPHY

Chapter 1

ANDREANO, RALPH L., ed., *The New Economic History: Recent Papers on Methodology.* New York: Wiley, 1970.

COCHRAN, THOMAS C., "Economic History, Old and New," *American Historical Review,* LXXIV (June 1969).

FISHLOW, ALBERT, and ROBERT W. FOGEL, "Quantitative Economic History: An Interim Evaluation, Past Trends and Present Tendencies," *Journal of Economic History,* XXXI (March 1971).

FOGEL, ROBERT WILLIAM, "The New Economic History: Its Findings and Methods," *Economic History Review,* XIX (Dec. 1966).

————, "The Specification Problem in Economic History," *Journal of Economic History,* XXVII (Sept. 1967).

————, "Historiography and Retrospective Econometrics," *History and Theory,* IX (1970).

HARTWELL, R. M., and ROBERT HIGGS, "Good Old Economic History," *American Historical Review,* LXXVI (April 1971).

MEYER, JOHN R., and ALFRED H. CONRAD, "Economic Theory, Statistical Inference, and Economic History," *Journal of Economic History,* XVII (Dec. 1957).

MURPHY, GEORGE G. S., "On Counterfactual Propositions," *History and Theory,* IX (1969).

NORTH, DOUGLAS C., "Economic History," in *International Encyclopedia of the Social Sciences.* New York: Crowell Collier and Macmillan, 1968.

WRIGHT, GAVIN, "Econometric Studies of History," in Michael D. Intriligator, ed., *Frontiers of Quantitative Economics.* London: North Holland, 1971.

Chapter 2

DAVIS, LANCE, and DOUGLASS C. NORTH, "Institutional Change and American Economic Growth: A First Step Towards a Theory of Institutional Innovation," *Journal of Economic History,* XXX (March 1970).

————, *Institutional Change and American Economic Growth.* Cambridge, England: Cambridge University Press, 1971.

HURST, JAMES WILLARD, *Law and the Conditions of Freedom in the Nineteenth-Century United States.* Madison: University of Wisconsin Press, 1956.

NORTH, DOUGLASS C., "Institutional Change and Economic Growth," *Journal of Economic History,* XXXI (March 1971).

Chapter 3

DAVIS, LANCE, and others, *American Economic Growth: An Economist's History of the United States.* New York: Harper, 1972.

FOGEL, ROBERT WILLIAM, and STANLEY L. ENGERMAN, eds., *The Reinterpretation of American Economic History.* New York: Harper, 1971.

GALLMAN, ROBERT E., "Commodity Output, 1839–1899," in National Bureau of Economic Research Conference on Research in Income and Wealth, *Trends in the American Economy in the Nineteenth Century.* New York: National Bureau of Economic Research, Inc., 1960.

———, "Gross National Product in the United States, 1834–1909," in National Bureau of Economic Research, Conference on Research in Income and Wealth, *Output, Employment, and Productivity in the United States after 1800.* New York: Columbia University Press, 1966.

———, "Trends in the Size Distribution of Wealth in the Nineteenth Century: Some Speculations," in National Bureau of Economic Research, Conference on Research in Income and Wealth, *Six Papers on the Size Distribution of Wealth and Income.* New York: Columbia University Press, 1969.

HIGGS, ROBERT, *The Transformation of the American Economy, 1865–1914: An Essay in Interpretation.* New York: Wiley, 1971.

KENDRICK, JOHN W., *Productivity Trends in the United States.* Princeton: Princeton University Press, 1961.

KUZNETS, SIMON, and others, *Population Redistribution and Economic Growth, United States, 1870–1950.* 3 vols. Philadelphia: American Philosophical Society, 1957–64.

LEBERGOTT, STANLEY, "Wage Trends, 1800–1900," in National Bureau of Economic Research Conference on Research in Income and Wealth, *Trends in the American Economy in the Nineteenth Century.* New York: National Bureau of Economic Research, Inc., 1960.

———, *Manpower in Economic Growth.* New York: McGraw-Hill, 1964.

———, "Labor Force and Employment, 1800–1960," in National Bureau of Economic Research, Conference on Research in Income and Wealth, *Output, Employment, and Productivity in the United States after 1800.* New York: Columbia University Press, 1966.

PERLOFF, HARVEY S., and others, *Regions, Resources, and Economic Growth.* Baltimore: Johns Hopkins Press, 1960.

SUTHERLAND, STELLA H., "Colonial Statistics," *Explorations in Entrepreneurial History,* V (Fall 1967).

U. S. Bureau of the Census, *Historical Statistics of the United States, Colonial Times to 1957.* Washington: Government Printing Office, 1960.

———, *Long-Term Economic Growth, 1860–1965.* Washington: Government Printing Office, 1966.

Chapters 4 and 5

ANDERSON, TERRY, *The Economic Growth of Seventeenth-Century New England: A Measurement of Regional Income.* Ph.D. dissertation, University of Washington, 1972.

BJORK, GORDON C., "The Weaning of the American Economy: Independence, Market Changes, and Economic Development," *Journal of Economic History,* XXIV (Dec. 1964).

DOMAR, EVSEY D., "The Causes of Slavery or Serfdom: A Hypothesis," *Journal of Economic History,* XXX (March 1970).

FISHLOW, ALBERT, "Discussion [of paper by Gordon C. Bjork]," *Journal of Economic History,* XXIV (Dec. 1964).

HARPER, LAWRENCE A., "The Effect of the Navigation Acts on the Thirteen Colonies," in R. B. Morris, ed., *The Era of the American Revolution.* New York: Columbia University Press, 1939.

JONES, ALICE HANSON, "Wealth Estimates for the American Middle Colonies, 1774," *Economic Development and Cultural Change,* XVIII (July 1970).

————, "Wealth Estimates for the New England Colonies about 1770," *Journal of Economic History,* XXXII (March 1972).

KLINGAMAN, DAVID, "Food Surpluses and Deficits in the American Colonies, 1768–1772," *Journal of Economic History,* XXXI (Sept. 1971).

McCLELLAND, PETER D., "The Cost to America of British Imperial Policy," *American Economic Review,* LIX (May 1969).

NORTH, DOUGLASS C., and ROBERT PAUL THOMAS, "An Economic Theory of the Growth of the Western World," *Economic History Review,* XXIII (April 1970).

————, "The Rise and Fall of the Manorial System: A Theoretical Model," *Journal of Economic History,* XXXI (Dec. 1971).

RANSOM, ROGER L, "British Policy and Colonial Growth: Some Implications of the Burden from the Navigation Acts," *Journal of Economic History,* XXVIII (Sept. 1968).

REID, JOSEPH D., "On Navigating the Navigation Acts with Peter D. McClelland: Comment," *American Economic Review,* LX (Dec. 1970).

SCOVILLE, WARREN C., "Did Colonial Farmers Waste Our Land?" *Southern Economic Journal,* XX (April 1953).

SHEPHERD, JAMES, "A Balance of Payments for the Thirteen Colonies, 1768–1772: A Summary," *Journal of Economic History,* XXV (Dec. 1965).

————, "Commodity Exports from the British North American Colonies to Overseas Areas, 1768–1772: Magnitudes and Patterns of Trade," *Explorations in Economic History,* VIII (Fall 1970).

————, and GARY M. WALTON, "Estimates of 'Invisible' Earnings in the Balance of Payments of the British North American Colonies, 1768–1772," *Journal of Economic History,* XXIX (June 1969).

————, "Trade, Distribution, and Economic Growth in Colonial America," *Journal of Economic History,* XXXII (March 1972).

————, *Shipping, Maritime Trade, and the Economic Development of Colonial North America* (Cambridge, England: Cambridge University Press, 1972).

THOMAS, ROBERT PAUL, "A Quantitative Approach to the Study of the Effects of British Imperial Policy upon Colonial Welfare: Some Preliminary Findings," *Journal of Economic History,* XXV (Dec. 1965).

————, "British Imperial Policy and the Economic Interpretation of the American Revolution," *Journal of Economic History,* XXVIII (Sept. 1968).

WALTON, GARY, "Sources of Productivity Change in American Colonial Shipping, 1675–1775," *Economic History Review,* XX (April 1967).

————, "New Evidence on Colonial Commerce," *Journal of Economic History,* XXVIII (Sept. 1968).

————, "The New Economic History and the Navigation Acts," *Economic History Review,* XXIV (Oct. 1971).

Chapter 6

DAVID, PAUL, "The Growth of Real Product in the United States Before 1840: New Evidence, Controlled Conjectures," *Journal of Economic History,* XXVII (June 1967).

————, "Learning by Doing and Tariff Protection: A Reconsideration of the Case of the Ante-Bellum United States Cotton Textile Industry," *Journal of Economic History,* XXX (Sept. 1970).

FOGEL, ROBERT WILLIAM, and STANLEY L. ENGERMAN, "A Model for the Explanation of Industrial Expansion during the Nineteenth Century: With an Application to the American Iron Industry," *Journal of Political Economy,* LXXVII (May/June 1969).

NORTH, DOUGLASS C., *The Economic Growth of the United States, 1790–1860.* Englewood Cliffs, N. J.: Prentice-Hall, 1961.

PARKER, WILLIAM N., and FRANKLEE WHARTENBY, "The Growth of Output before 1840," in National Bureau of Economic Research, Conference on Research in Income and Wealth, *Trends in the American Economy in the Nineteenth Century.* Princeton: Princeton University Press, 1960.

ROSTOW, W. W., *The Stages of Economic Growth: A Non-Communist Manifesto.* Cambridge, England: Cambridge University Press, 1960.

————, ed., *The Economics of Take-off into Sustained Growth.* New York: St. Martin's Press, 1964.

TEMIN, PETER, "The Causes of Cotton-Price Fluctuations in the 1830's," *Review of Economics and Statistics,* IL (Nov. 1967).

————, *The Jacksonian Economy.* New York: Norton, 1969.

WRIGHT, GAVIN, "An Econometric Study of Cotton Production and Trade, 1830–1860," *Review of Economics and Statistics,* LIII (May 1971).

Chapter 7

ANDREANO, RALPH L., ed., *The Economic Impact of the American Civil War,* 2d ed. Cambridge, Mass.: Schenkman, 1967.

BECKER, GARY S., *The Economics of Discrimination.* Chicago: University of Chicago Press, 1957).

CONRAD, ALFRED H., and JOHN R. MEYER, "The Economics of Slavery in the Ante-Bellum South," *Journal of Political Economy,* LXVI (April 1958).

EASTERLIN, RICHARD A., "Regional Income Trends, 1840–1950," in Seymour E. Harris, ed., *American Economic History.* New York: McGraw-Hill, 1961.

ENGERMAN, STANLEY L., "Some Economic Factors in Southern Backwardness in the Nineteenth Century," in John F. Kain and John R. Meyer, eds., *Essays in Regional Economics.* Cambridge, Mass.: Harvard University Press, 1971.

EVANS, ROBERT, JR., "The Economics of American Negro Slavery," in H. Gregg Lewis, ed., *Aspects of Labor Economics.* Princeton: Princeton University Press, 1962.

FOGEL, ROBERT WILLIAM, and STANLEY L. ENGERMAN, "The Relative Efficiency of Slavery: A Comparison of Northern and Southern Agriculture in 1860," *Explorations in Economic History,* VIII (Spring 1971).

HIGGS, ROBERT, "Did Southern Farmers Discriminate?" *Agricultural History,* XLVI (April 1972).

————, "Race, Tenure, and Resource Allocation in Southern Agriculture, 1910," *Journal of Economic History,* XXXIII (March 1973).

HUTCHINSON, WILLIAM K., and SAMUEL H. WILLIAMSON, "The Self-Sufficiency of the Antebellum South: Estimates of the Food Supply," *Journal of Economic History,* XXXI (Sept. 1971).

PARKER, WILLIAM N., ed., *The Structure of the Cotton Economy of the Antebellum South.* Washington: Agricultural History Society, 1970.

SOLOMON, LEWIS, "Estimates of the Costs of Schooling in 1880 and 1890," *Explorations in Economic History,* VII (Supplement 1970).

STAROBIN, ROBERT, "The Economics of Industrial Slavery in the Old South," *Business History Review,* XLIV (Summer 1970).

SUTCH, RICHARD, "The Profitability of Ante-Bellum Slavery—Revisited," *Southern Economic Journal,* XXXI (April 1965).

YASUBA, YASUKICHI, "The Profitability and Viability of Plantation Slavery in the United States," *Economic Studies Quarterly,* XII (Sept. 1961).

Chapter 8

DAVIS, LANCE E., and JOHN LEGLER, "The Government in the American Economy, 1815–1902: A Quantitative Study," *Journal of Economic History,* XXVI (Dec. 1966).

FISHLOW, ALBERT, "Levels of Nineteenth-Century Investment in Education," *Journal of Economic History,* XXVI (Dec. 1966).

FOGEL, ROBERT WILLIAM, *The Union Pacific Railroad: A Case in Premature Enterprise.* Baltimore: Johns Hopkins Press, 1960.

GOODRICH, CARTER, "Internal Improvements Reconsidered," *Journal of Economic History,* XXX (June 1970).

GRILICHES, ZVI, "Research Costs and Social Returns: Hybrid Corn and Related Innovations," *Journal of Political Economy,* LXVI (Oct. 1958).

MACAVOY, PAUL W., *The Economic Effects of Regulation: The Trunk-Line Railroad Cartels and the Interstate Commerce Commission before 1900.* Cambridge, Mass.: M.I.T. Press, 1965.

SCHULTZ, THEODORE W., *The Economic Organization of Agriculture.* New York: McGraw-Hill, 1953.

SYLLA, RICHARD, "Federal Policy, Banking Market Structure, and Capital Mobilization in the United States, 1863–1913," *Journal of Economic History,* XXIX (Dec. 1969).

Chapter 9

BOYD, J. HAYDEN, and GARY M. WALTON, "The Social Savings from Nineteenth-Century Rail Passenger Services," *Explorations in Economic History,* IX (Spring 1972).

DAVID, PAUL A., "Transport Innovation and Economic Growth," *Economic History Review,* XXII (Dec. 1969).

FISHLOW, ALBERT, *Railroads and the Transformation of the Ante-Bellum Economy* Cambridge, Mass.: Harvard University Press, 1965.

——, "Productivity and Technological Change in the Railroad Sector 1838–1899," in National Bureau of Economic Research Conference on Research in Income and Wealth, *Output, Employment, and Productivity in the United States after 1800.* New York: National Bureau of Economic Research, Inc., 1966.

FOGEL, ROBERT WILLIAM, *Railroads and American Economic Growth: Essays in Econometric History.* Baltimore: Johns Hopkins Press, 1964.

GOODRICH, CARTER, and others, *Canals and American Economic Growth*. New York: Columbia University Press, 1960.

HAITES, ERICK F. and JAMES MAK, "Ohio and Mississippi River Transportation, 1810–1860," *Explorations in Economic History*, VIII (Winter 1970–71).

LEBERGOTT, STANLEY, "United States Transport Advance and Externalities," *Journal of Economic History*, XXVI (Dec. 1966).

McCLELLAND, PETER D., "Railroads, American Growth, and the New Economic History: A Critique," *Journal of Economic History*, XXVIII (March 1968).

MERCER, LLOYD J., "Land Grants to American Railroads: Social Cost or Social Benefit," *Business History Review*, XLIII (Summer 1969).

———, "Maximum Bias in Social Saving Estimates Using Prices," *American Economic Review*, LX (March 1970).

———, "Rates of Return for Land-Grant Railroads: The Central Pacific System," *Journal of Economic History*, XXX (Sept. 1970).

NORTH, DOUGLASS C., "Ocean Freight Rates and Economic Development, 1750–1913," *Journal of Economic History*, XVIII (Dec. 1958).

———, "The Role of Transportation in the Economic Development of North America," in *Les grandes voies dans le monde, XVe-XIXe siècles* (Paris: SEVPEN, 1965).

———, "Sources of Productivity Change in Ocean Shipping, 1600–1850," *Journal of Political Economy*, LXXVI (Sept./Oct. 1968).

RANSOM, ROGER L., "Canals and Development: A Discussion of the Issues," *American Economic Review*, LIV (May 1964).

———, "Interregional Canals and Economic Specialization in the Antebellum United States," *Explorations in Entrepreneurial History*, V (Fall 1967).

———, "Social Returns from Public Transport Investment: A Case Study of the Ohio Canal," *Journal of Political Economy*, LXXVIII (Sept./Oct. 1970).

Chapter 10

ENGERMAN, STANLEY L., "Some Economic Issues Relating to Railroad Subsidies and the Evaluation of Land Grants," *Journal of Economic History*, XXXII (June 1972).

FOGEL, ROBERT WILLIAM, and JACK RUTNER, "The Efficiency Effects of Federal Land Policy, 1850–1900: A Report of Some Provisional Findings," in William Aydelotte and others, eds., *Dimensions of Quantitative Research in History*. Princeton: Princeton University Press, 1972.

PASSELL, PETER, "The Impact of Cotton Land Distribution on the Antebellum Economy," *Journal of Economic History*, XXXI (Dec. 1971).

———, and MARIA SCHMUNDT, "Pre-Civil War Land Policy and the Growth of Manufacturing," *Explorations in Economic History*, IX (Fall 1971).

Chapter 11

BOGUE, ALLAN G., *Money at Interest: The Farm Mortgage on the Middle Border* (Ithaca: Cornell University Press, 1955).

———, *From Prairie to Corn Belt: Farming on the Illinois and Iowa Prairies in the Nineteenth Century* (Chicago: University of Chicago Press, 1963).

———, and MARGARET B. BOGUE, " 'Profits' and the Frontier Land Speculator," *Journal of Economic History*, XVII (March 1957).

BOWMAN, JOHN D., "An Economic Analysis of Midwestern Farm Land Values and Farm Land Income, 1860 to 1900," *Yale Economic Essays*, V (Fall 1965).

FISHER, FRANKLIN M., and PETER TEMIN, "Regional Specialization and the Supply of Wheat in the United States, 1867–1914," *Review of Economics and Statistics*, LII (May 1970).

HIGGS, ROBERT, "Railroad Rates and the Populist Uprising," *Agricultural History*, XLIV (July 1970).

———, "Regional Specialization and the Supply of Wheat in the United States, 1867–1914: A Comment," *Review of Economics and Statistics*, LIII (Feb. 1971).

LURIE, JONATHAN, "Speculation, Risk, and Profits: The Ambivalent Agrarian in the Late Nineteenth Century," *Agricultural History*, XLVI (April 1972).

MAYHEW, ANNE, "A Reappraisal of the Causes of Farm Protest in the United States, 1870–1900," *Journal of Economic History*, XXXII (June 1972).

NUGENT, WALTER T. K., "Some Parameters of Populism," *Agricultural History*, XL (Oct. 1966).

PARKER, WILLIAM N., "Sources of Agricultural Productivity in the Nineteenth Century," *Journal of Farm Economics*, IL (Dec. 1967).

———, and JUDITH L. V. KLEIN, "Productivity Growth in Grain Production in the United States, 1840–60 and 1900–10," in National Bureau of Economic Research Conference on Research in Income and Wealth, *Output, Employment, and Productivity in the United States after 1800*. New York: Columbia University Press, 1966.

RASMUSSEN, WAYNE D., "The Impact of Technological Change on American Agriculture, 1862–1962," *Journal of Economic History*, XXII (Dec. 1962).

ROTHSTEIN, MORTON, "America in the International Rivalry for the British Wheat Market," *Mississippi Valley Historical Review*, XLVII (Dec. 1960).

SWIERENGA, ROBERT P., "Land Speculator 'Profits' Reconsidered: Central Iowa As a Test Case," *Journal of Economic History*, XXVI (March 1966).

———, *Pioneers and Profits: Land Speculation of the Iowa Frontier*. Ames: Iowa State University Press, 1968.

Chapter 12

DAVIS, LANCE, "The Investment Market, 1870–1914: The Evolution of a National Market," *Journal of Economic History*, XXV (Sept. 1965).

FELS, RENDIGS, *American Business Cycles, 1865–1897* (Chapel Hill: University of North Carolina Press, 1959).

HIGGS, ROBERT, "The Growth of Cities in a Midwestern Region, 1870–1900," *Journal of Regional Science*, IX (Dec. 1969).

———, "American Inventiveness, 1870–1920," *Journal of Political Economy*, LXXIX (May/June 1971).

———, "Race, Skills, and Earnings: American Immigrants in 1909," *Journal of Economic History*, XXXI (June 1971).

———, "Cities and Yankee Ingenuity, 1870–1920," in Kenneth T. Jackson and Stanley Schultz, eds., *Cities in American History*. New York: Knopf, 1972.

LONG, CLARENCE, *Wages and Earnings in the United States, 1860–1890*. Princeton: Princeton University Press, 1960.

MEEKER, EDWARD F., *The Economics of Improving Health, 1850–1915*. Ph.D. dissertation, University of Washington, 1970.

———, "The Improving Health of the United States, 1850–1915," *Explorations in Economic History*, IX (Summer 1972).

PRED, ALLAN R., *The Spatial Dynamics of U. S. Urban-Industrial Growth, 1800–1914.* Cambridge, Mass.: M.I.T. Press, 1966.

REES, ALBERT, *Real Wages in Manufacturing, 1890–1914.* Princeton: Princeton University Press, 1961.

ROSENBERG, NATHAN, "Technological Change in the Machine Tool Industry, 1840–1910," *Journal of Economic History,* XXIII (Dec. 1963).

————, ed., *The American System of Manufactures.* Edinburgh: Edinburgh University Press, 1969.

————, *Technology and American Economic Growth.* New York: Harper, 1972.

SCHMOOKLER, JACOB, *Invention and Economic Growth.* Cambridge, Mass.: Harvard University Press, 1966.

TEMIN, PETER, *Iron and Steel in Nineteenth-Century America: An Economic Inquiry.* Cambridge, Mass.: M.I.T. Press, 1964.

THOMAS, ROBERT PAUL, "The Automobile Industry and Its Tycoon," *Explorations in Entrepreneurial History* VI (Winter 1969).

Chapters 13 and 14

ADAMS, WALTER, "The Military-Industrial Complex and the New Industrial State," *American Economic Review,* LVIII (May 1968).

BARNETT, HAROLD J., and CHANDLER MORSE, *Scarcity and Growth: The Economics of Natural Resource Availability.* Baltimore: Johns Hopkins Press, 1963.

BROWN, E. CARY, "Fiscal Policy in the 'Thirties: A Reappraisal," *American Economic Review,* XLVI (Dec. 1956).

CHANDLER, LESTER V., *America's Greatest Depression, 1929–1941.* New York: Harper, 1970.

CLAYTON, JAMES L., ed., *The Economic Impact of the Cold War.* New York: Harcourt, 1970.

FRIEDMAN, MILTON, and ANNA J. SCHWARTZ, *A Monetary History of the United States, 1867–1960* (Princeton: Princeton University Press, 1963).

KRAVIS, IRVING B., "Relative Income Shares in Fact and Theory," *American Economic Review,* XLIX (Dec. 1959).

KUZNETS, SIMON, assisted by ELIZABETH JENKS, *Shares of Upper Income Groups in Income and Saving.* New York: National Bureau of Economic Research, 1953.

LAMPMAN, ROBERT J., *The Share of Top Wealth-Holders in National Wealth, 1922–1956.* Princeton: Princeton University Press, 1962.

MOORE, GEOFFREY H., "Secular Changes in the Distribution of Income," *American Economic Review,* XLII (March 1952).

VATTER, HAROLD G., *The U. S. Economy in the 1950's.* New York: Norton, 1963.

INDEX

A

Agrarian discontent, 130–39
  protest movements, 130
  role of farm prices, 11
  Shays' Rebellion, 61
  sources of, 11, 134–37
Agricultural Adjustment Act, 161
Agricultural labor force,
  distribution of, in
  nineteenth century, 33
Agricultural lands, new, 41
Agricultural output:
  demand, and the westward
    movement, 122
  effects of railroads, 113–15
  sources of, 138
  terms of trade, 1865–1900
    (chart), 131
Agriculture:
  in Colonial America, 49–50
  expansion in West, 31
  farmers as land speculators, 121
  government research in, 102–4
  impact of railroad on relocation
    of, 113

monopolistic practices and,
    130–31
  new land put into farms
    (chart), 139
  price support program, 167
  total factor productivity,
    1869–1955 (chart), 139
Allocation of resources, and role of
  government in, 163
American colonists, welfare under
  British rule, 13
American Federation of Labor,
  43, 166
American Revolution, causes of,
  53–56
Anderson, Terry, 84
Appalachian Mountains, 52, 74
Argentina, in international wheat
  market, 135
Articles of Confederation, 62
Australia, in international wheat
  market, 135
Automobiles:
  development, 44
  durable goods industry, 156
  major impact on economy, 144
  manufacturing, 144–46
  output of passenger motor
    vehicles, 1899–1938

F

Q

V

W

U